• •

I Survived a House Fire...
I Wish My Stuff Had

*How to prepare for and survive a devastating
event with more than memories*

by Candace Quinn

iUniverse, Inc.
New York   Bloomington

I Survived A House Fire... I Wish My Stuff Had
How to prepare for and survive a devastating event with more than memories
Copyright © 2008 by Candace A. Quinn

The information, ideas, and suggestions in this book are not intended to render professional advice. Before following any suggestions contained in this book, you should consult your personal accountant, insurance agent, or other financial advisor. Neither the author nor the publisher shall be liable or responsible for any loss or damage allegedly arising as a consequence of your use or application of any information or suggestions in this book.

iUniverse books may be ordered through booksellers or by contacting:

iUniverse
1663 Liberty Drive
Bloomington, IN 47403
www.iuniverse.com
1-800-Authors (1-800-288-4677)

Because of the dynamic nature of the Internet, any Web addresses or links contained in this book may have changed since publication and may no longer be valid. The views expressed in this work are solely those of the author and do not necessarily reflect the views of the publisher, and the publisher hereby disclaims any responsibility for them.

ISBN: 978-0-595-51842-5 (pbk)
ISBN: 978-0-595-62057-9 (ebk)

Printed in the United States of America

Dedicated to my loving husband, Michael, who always brings his sense of humor to every situation;

To Dad, Chris, Gabe, Noah, Greg, and Jim, the firefighters in my family; and, to the all the men and women of the Longmeadow Fire Department who came to our rescue.

CONTENTS

. . . .

INTRODUCTION: OUR STORY

Forty-eight years of stuff married forty-one years of stuff, and it all fit nicely into an eighty-year-old, quaint New England Colonial, nestled into a quiet neighborhood of a delightful bedroom community, with homes tucked onto long narrow lots, putting houses about twenty feet apart. We were tired from too many time zones in too few days, a hectic work schedule, late days, and not enough sleep. We just wanted to sleep until noon the next morning. Our home, however, had other ideas. At 3:10 AM our world changed forever.

My husband and I had just returned home to New England from a magical storybook wedding and honeymoon that had us spending a week in California and three weeks in Tahiti. We had just moved his belongings into my home of thirteen years, and we were returning to our work lives. It was Friday, May 8—a glorious night. We were getting a glimpse of New England's promise of spring, and we had thrown open the second story windows to allow us to sleep with the crisp fresh air an early May evening can bring. As we ascended the winding, painted, and stenciled wood staircase to our room, I hesitated at the landing and asked my husband if he smelled smoke. It was 9 PM. He said no, it's probably a neighbor's wood burning fireplace. Let's just go to sleep. He instructed me to not disturb him for anything; he was sleeping until noon.

My instincts had me turn around and do a final check on that old house. Back on the first floor, we had secured the windows and locked the doors, and nothing seemed out of the ordinary. Our dogs were quiet and slumbering in their basement headquarters. So I decided to join them in their repose, returning to the second floor bedroom, where I found my husband was fast asleep.

I've tried many times to recall just what it was that awakened me at 3:10 AM, and I am satisfied that it was my guardian angel gently whispering, "Wake up,

1

now, *you must wake up.* ". I only recall sitting straight up in bed and thinking, "What is that orange light in the window?" as I gazed in a dreamy, yet startled, state around the bedroom. All three windows were aglow in eerie neon orange. My husband later informed me that I said, "Honey, what is that sound?" as I shook him out of his sleep. He awoke to a start, thinking an intruder was breaking a first floor window as he recalls hearing the shattering of glass. We quickly abandoned the security of our bed and hurried to peer out one of those orange windows. Our first—still not quite awake—observation was that we were seeing fire; a wall of fire in fact. Nothing was computing. It must be the house next door since there was no smoke in our house. Yet, we could feel the heat of the flames that were licking at those very windows. Even with all those windows open, there was no smoke in our house. There was no smoke alarm going off to sound any type of alarm. I kept thinking, it must be something else. I grabbed the bedroom phone and dialed 9-1-1, while my husband ran out of the bedroom, calling out that he would get the dogs and urging me to get out of the house quickly.

Within a few moments, we reunited in our back yard, where we found the side porch under our bedroom completely ablaze. As I gazed around, anxiously awaiting a siren, I saw our dogs wandering the back yard, confused. I realized we had not grabbed their leashes in our hurry to escape. Now, at this time, my husband was standing about ten feet away from the burning porch, holding the garden hose in his hands. He was trying to understand why now, of all the times possible, there was no water pressure (when in reality, the fire was so hot; the water was evaporating as quickly as it left the hose). I told him that I was going back into the house to grab the dog leashes; they were just inside the door. Upon re-entering, I ran into a wall of choking, blinding smoke and heard the sounds of our smoke detectors alerting us to trouble. No kidding! Fortunately the leashes were reachable without leaving the security of the door landing and threshold; however, nothing else was: not my wedding rings back upstairs on the nightstand; not my glasses on the same nightstand; neither a pair of shoes nor a jacket for my barefoot, t-shirt-clad husband—nothing.

And so, my husband and I watched a merciless fire consume our home and belongings rapidly. The fire department arrived in moments, able only to focus on saving the adjacent home. The fire department chaplain immediately began preparing us for the worst. I wish we had been prepared.

What remained of the staircase we descended

I come from a family of firefighters. My Dad was a volunteer for years, and my brother joined as a cadet as soon as he was able, at age sixteen. At the time of our fire, he was a Deputy Chief with the fire department in my hometown in northern Illinois. Most of my cousins have all volunteered at one point or another, and, like their dad, my two nephews are both career, full-time firefighters. Imagine my brother's heartfelt anguish when I called him at 5 AM that Saturday, from a thousand miles away, to tell him what was happening. Rightfully, he took the only position a firefighter can take, "Thank God you and Mike are OK. Everything will be ok."

I thought he was crazy. (A frequent thought I have about my only sibling). I was in shock. I was overwhelmed. Neighbors were giving us their coats to stay warm—we were in our pajamas—and the young man next-door even came out and gave my husband his brand new sneakers. The Red Cross was in front of my house. I was our neighborhood disaster! How could this be happening to me? To us? I was on the board of directors of the local chapter of the American Red Cross. I raised money for people in this situation. This can't be happening to me! This is my home—the place where I am safe. This only happens to other people—you know, the ones you see on the news!

And there they were, right in front of my house: the TV news trucks. Reporters from each local station had arrived. The weekend anchors had come out of their comfortable beds to cover this big fire. These were people I knew. I worked in Public Relations and talked to these guys all the time. There were people gathering from everywhere. I learned later that one neighbor went inside his home and came back out with a video camera and proceeded to document the fire.

3

I just kept recognizing how overwhelmed I felt. Then my daughter and son-in-law arrived, comforted us, and said not to worry. We could stay with them as long as we needed. They immediately took our dogs back to their house, just fifteen minutes away, to protect them from the chaos, and then returned to ours.

By dawn, the fire was under control. The roof was gone; the third floor fully exposed. The fire had gutted the entire third floor, half of the second floor, and half of the first floor, but the worst of it was over. Friends of ours began to gather, wanting to help. They waited to see what form that should take. A realtor friend immediately began looking for housing for us as an interim solution. By noon, we had salvaged what photos we could locate and our dear friends took these to their homes to clean, dry, and hope for the best. Another friend who worked for a fire restoration company had been with us since 5 AM, and he was talking to my insurance company. I was overwhelmed. (This would become my word for several months to come).

Also by noon, my daughter had found basic clothing for us. We had showered and were looking at a possible rental our realtor friend located (In less than four hours, she had found this in a community that has roughly two vacancies a year). We had food arriving, and our friend with the fire restoration company was gathering supplies so that we could go safely into the house to begin the process of recovery. So much kindness, so much compassion, I was overwhelmed.

It wasn't until three weeks later that my pity party and sense of total confusion about what to do ended. I awoke that particular morning in our still foreign rental house, in a rented bed, and turned on our rented television. There was a story on the news about a house fire that occurred the night before in a neighboring town. This time it was a two-family home. Two young children had perished. A single mother was sobbing, and the authorities were taking her nine-year-old child into protective custody. It appeared that the children's mother had left them home unattended and this oldest child had started the fire. I began to reflect. I was overwhelmed, yet I had lost only possessions. Things. This woman on the news had truly lost all *her possessions; her two young children had lost their lives; and now the authorities had taken her oldest child because he was somehow the cause of this devastation.* Who was I to be overwhelmed? *Look at all I had. What I lost was just stuff. I still had my husband and my family. I still had our life together and our beautiful, loving friends. I still had my memories. What more did I need?*

As you read this book, know that in the scheme of life, this was a major event. But even more amazing is that now, after six years, it feels more like a lesson than a life-changing event. Perspective is an amazing thing.

I decided that day to chronicle the lessons I learned, and to document for others the discoveries I was making as I searched for information on building a fire-safe home. This book is the result of lessons learned, observations made, research conducted, advice received, and the desire to pass along the information everyone— renter, homeowner, boarder—needs to know: how to prepare to protect yourself, your loved ones, and your belongings from devastation. You can take precautions, make enhancements, store, stash, and file things differently. You can plan, practice, and protect yourself and your family. So read, learn, and take action.

How to use this book:

When you see this symbol, 🐾, you'll be getting information that applies to your entire home, not just the room in which the suggestion has been covered.

This symbol, 🧯, indicates that the information that will follow represents what to do in the event of fire.

This symbol, 💡, indicates that key lessons or tips are in this list.

Chapter One: Getting Started

In May of 2006, CBS Morning News reported that every eighty seconds, there is a report of a house fire[1], and many of these are preventable. Another substantial percentage of people sustain losses that some advanced preparation might have lessened. Fire is the third leading cause of unintentional death in the home, behind poisoning and falls. Fully, 80 percent of all fire-related deaths occur in a home, with 85 percent of these in single-family homes.[2] That's right. Right here in our personal sanctuaries. Right here, where *nothing* is supposed to happen to us. The objective of this book is to help you prepare yourself, your family, and your home in the event of a disaster.

We'll begin by discussing general fire safety in new construction design, followed by renovation considerations. Then we'll move inside and look room by room at dangers, precautions, and preservation steps you may want to consider. We'll then look to our favorite places to store, collect, and stash things. Finally, I'll offer you some suggestions for preparing to file a claim. I've included a spread sheet in Appendix B that I created for my claim, but it can also serve as a system for recording current inventory and documenting your home. As with any situation, the best defense is a good offense. I hope you'll take this time to go room by room with me and take the actions needed to protect your home, your belongings, and your life.

 Document

Begin by grabbing your camera and taking photos of everything—not eBay-for-sale quality—but as a means of documenting your furnishings and belongings. Photograph the walls, the shelves, the cupboards, the floors, the closets, the furniture, the appliances—everything. Then, print a set of pictures, and store them anywhere *but* your home. The time to figure out what you own is not while you are filing a claim. Once a year, repeat this process and give a copy to your insurance agent. Then, should you ever need to file a claim, you'll both start from the same page.

Documentation: Items > $100

Step 1   Take a picture of each item.

Step 2   Keep original dated receipts, and record make & model/serial number of item where available.

Step 3   Put both the receipt and the photo in a small zippered plastic bag.

Step 4   Store in a fire-rated file or safe. I suggest you file these in folders, by location in your home.

Step 5   Repeat steps 1-4 after every new purchase.

Step 6   Periodically review these files to weed out items you've discarded.

Insurance Tips

While we're talking about insurance, this is an opportune time to mention things you'll want to talk to your agent about. Renter's insurance is a must if you board or rent. This policy generally covers your belongings in a casualty loss situation, up to a limit. Typically, a renter's policy covers between $10,000 and $25,000 in furnishings and clothing, etc. If you have art, jewelry, or other collectibles, you'll want to discuss this separately with your agent and likely he/she will encourage you to consider a "rider".

Homeowner's insurance generally includes multiple elements: liability (not a topic we'll cover here), medical (also not covered here), property, and contents. Most of us spend the greatest amount of time selecting insurance when we first purchase our homes. In order to obtain a mortgage, most lenders require, at a minimum, coverage that equals or exceeds the amount of the mortgage. Left to our own devices, most people don't think about this enough. A good agent will have a conversation with you at least every other year, taking into consideration property values, improvements, additions, etc., to determine if your current coverage and elections are still sufficient for your needs.

Most homeowner's policies insure your belongings under the property section using a percentage of the home's insured value to set the coverage limits. So, if you purchase your home for $100,000, and it is on a lot with an assessed value of $15,000, then your homeowner's policy should be $85,000. (This is only an example. You will want to discuss with your agent not only your investment but also your replacement considerations). Your belongings—your clothes, shoes, furniture, tools, toys, etc.—will be covered in the event of a loss up to some percentage of that $85,000, usually 70-80 percent. "Replacement" value is usually fine, if you only lose one room; but in the case of a total loss like we had, replacement value meant once the loss amount equaled 80 percent of the home's insured amount, our recovery stopped. Since this was my first home, purchased over thirteen years prior to the fire, the value of our combined belongings had surpassed the 80 percent value of the insured house. The lessons we learned were to cover our antiques, jewelry, furs, major equipment, and art under a separate rider; to make sure insurance amounts are adequate not only to rebuild but also to replace; and to have your home reappraised periodically, depending upon the local market, to assure coverage at current housing levels.

A good, qualified, (certified, licensed, or credentialed) insurance agent is critical to your security. Understand your coverage and your loss detail. Every policy clearly delineates your coverage for fire, smoke, water, wind, and all types of casualties, due to acts of nature or man. The amount of coverage, the type of coverage, and your personal risk rating (which is a function of your experience and past claims) are key drivers insurance companies use to determine your rates.

As we go through the house, I suggest you consider the "Prevention, Preservation, and Safety Shopping List" in Appendix A. You may want some of these items right away as we take this journey to prepare your home. At a minimum, take a pen and either a small pad of paper or this book—designed to help you journal your thoughts as you go—with you and start your list of what you'll grab when someone says, "You've got ten minutes to get out of your house! What do you want to save?"

I also recommend that you make a list, in order of importance, of the ten things you could not imagine your life without. (Appendix C is available for this purpose). As we go through the house, you may consider storing these things differently or even pre-packing them in tubs to grab-and-go. Let's begin with some basics on prevention.

 **Key Lessons:**

1. Document what you own, what it cost, when you acquired it, and take pictures of everything.

2. Keep these records in a location *not* within your home.

3. Re-photograph every room, every closet, every cupboard, and every drawer, every other year.

4. Be sure you have adequate home insurance and revisit your coverage at least every two years.

● ● ● ● ● ● ● ● ● ● ● ● ● ● ● ● ● ● ● ●

CHAPTER TWO: PREVENTION AND SAFETY

Nationwide, there is a home fire death every 204 minutes.[3] Let's begin our discussion with a look at prevention and safety. There are steps you can take to protect yourself and your loved ones if disaster strikes.

RACE

RACE: This word is the key to guiding your actions upon discovering a fire. It will save your life and those of the ones you love. RACE stands for: Rescue, Alert, Confine, and Extinguish.

It bears repeating: Rescue, Alert, Confine, and Extinguish. In that order! First and foremost, *find everyone in your home*. Call out, make noise, and get all of your loved ones—and pets—out of danger. This means out of the building to the gathering space you identified ahead of time, away from the fire, and out of the way of rescue teams. *Then alert the fire department.* If the only phone you can use to call the fire department remains attached to the building that's on fire, be sure to tell the operator this information. The fire department only needs an address to take action, but they like to keep you on the phone—if it's safe—in order to make certain that they have successfully found you. They do, however, want you safely away from any danger. *Confine the fire* to its immediate area if at all possible. Move rugs, furnishings, and any loose items away from the area, if it is safe to do so. Close the door to the area involved, and remove any source of fuels. Then, if it feels safe, *extinguish the fire* if possible. If you are not making progress within one minute, get out. Let the professionals do their work.

Early Warning Devices

Experts report that 65 percent of home fire deaths occur in homes without smoke alarms.[4] For pennies a day, you can install a hard-wired home security system—with battery backup units—with fire, CO, and water alarms in addition to the expected intruder alert. *These systems require installation by qualified, licensed electricians.* When triggered, such a system will not only alert occupants, but will also dial emergency services in your area. This leaves you free to rescue and evacuate.

REMEMBER

When you change your clocks, change your smoke alarm batteries and test your alarm systems.

Smoke alarms are the residential fire safety success story of the past quarter century. The technology has been around since the 1960s, but the single station, battery-powered smoke alarm we have today became available to consumers in the 1970s, and the National Fire Protection Association (herein referenced as NFPA) estimates that 96 percent of U.S. homes have at least one smoke alarm today.[5]

These alarms should be placed, at a minimum, outside entrances to each bedroom (and inside if you sleep with the door closed), in the halls near the laundry and furnace rooms, and at least one in each stairwell, on every floor in the house (including the basement). Garages, whether attached or detached, should also have working alarms. If feasible, install a heat sensor in your attic and garage as well. Remember that smoke rises, so if you have vaulted ceilings, place your alarms at the highest point.

Don't install alarms near windows, outside doors, or in front of ducts where drafts can interfere with the smoke detection. Never paint your smoke alarms or decorate them in any way. They are a safety item, not a design statement. Paint and other decorations can interfere with their operation.

You *do* need to maintain these devices. I'm lucky. My brother, the firefighter, travels a thousand miles to see me twice a year and I'm sure it is, in part, just to service my smoke alarms. So, if you don't have a firefighter family member looking out for you, you'll have to do this yourself. At a minimum, you should service your alarms as follows:

Smoke Alarms[6]

1. Test them, once a month.

2. Clean, dust and vacuum them.

3. Change batteries every six months. A great rule of thumb is when you change your clocks, change your battery.

4. Replace the alarm every seven to ten years, based upon manufacturer's recommendations.

5. Never borrow a battery from the smoke alarm. Today could be the day you need the alert!

6. If anyone in the household is hearing impaired, be sure to purchase models that feature a strobe light and have under pillow vibration alerts.

To obtain a list of manufacturers that distribute alarms to the hearing impaired, contact the NFPA's Center for High Risk Outreach.

Several alarm systems feature low voltage monitored systems (inexpensive to purchase and operate). Dual sensor systems, considered to be the best design, feature an ionization element for rapid fire detection as well as a photo electric sensor to detect slow smoldering fires (like the one I experienced). Ideally, select a combination system with a photo electric alarm for every twenty feet of kitchen and bath space, and one of each for the cellar and attic. Be sure both of these areas contain heat sensors as well. [7]

In addition, most vendors have systems that also detect water. An overflowing toilet can flood a home in just a few short hours, much less time than your normal workday or a great shopping trip! I can assure you that nothing ruins a vacation quicker than a call from a neighbor that there is water gushing out of your front door!

Finally, every home should also have a CO detector and alarm (carbon monoxide—that silent killer!) and if appropriate, a natural gas detector and alarm.

 **Practice Your Escape**

In every season, have an escape plan. Write it down. Draw a picture. Practice it. Regularly.

We were lucky. Our fire started on the outside of our house. We were extremely lucky that something awakened us and neither smoke, heat, nor fire blocked our escape. I remember getting outside safely, observing my husband with the garden hose, and watching our poor dogs who were dazed and confused. I remember going back into the house not more than three steps, feeling the heat, and hitting that smoke! It was so thick, so choking. How did that happen so fast? It had only been minutes, seconds earlier when we descended those same stairs with no smoke.

Start your plan with how to get out. Ok, doors are obvious but not always your safest way out. Practice by putting a red towel in a spot to represent the fire barrier. Make sure your family, young and old alike, know what the alternatives are in the event fire blocks an exit.

This means having family members practice using windows as an escape. This may seem silly, but have each family member begin by practicing unlocking, opening, and closing every home window. Can they remove storm windows from the inside? What about the screens? Can they identify something at hand that might help them break the window if it's too smoky to take the time to do the locks, raise the window, and remove the storm? Do you have family members who are just too small or too weak to perform these tasks? Know this ahead of time, and have a plan.

While on the subject of windows, this is a great time to talk about fire escape ladders for second and third story escapes. There are several vendors of approved fire escape ladders on the market. Once you've selected the ladder that works best for your situation, be sure to discover before a fire whether every member of your family can lift and install this ladder. If not, assign someone to go help the person unable to use it. At a minimum, you need one ladder per upper level floor, but the safest approach is to have one in each bedroom, on each floor. I keep ours at the foot of each bed in a small chest. They are out of site, but immediately available. The ladder is the only thing in these chests. By doing this, there is no clutter to dig through, so that in an emergency, that lifeline of escape is readily accessible. One vendor sells a model you can install into the wall between the studs directly under the window—a great idea. Now no one has to carry it over to the window. *Practice using this ladder at least once.*

It was my firefighter brother, of course, who gave me my first set of ladders as a Christmas gift many years ago. My school-aged children and I were living in an apartment on the third floor of a walk- up, in an older section of a great college

13

community. The kids' bedrooms were at the rear of the building, and they shared a porch that overlooked our secured back yard. When my brother came to visit that following spring, he asked me if we had practiced using the ladder yet. Well, I am very afraid of heights, so of course, we had not practiced. He proceeded to take the children onto the porch, remove the ladder from its chest, and had each child open the window, lift the screen, attach the ladder, and then with him going down in front of them, they each practiced descending the ladder. They were proud and confident that they could do this if they had to. I couldn't watch, but I did sleep better that night knowing that, if they had to, my kids could escape.

If you live in a condominium, or other dwelling, with more than three floors, encourage your building management to have drills where you and your family can practice an escape.

And while it feels cruel and unusual, do an alarm test after the family is asleep one weekend evening, and determine if the alarm is capable of waking each family member. Don't wait for a real disaster to learn that dad or your teenager will sleep through this, especially if mom is away and the kids are counting on dad or that teenager.

💡 About Keyed Deadbolts

- Great for anti-theft.
- Bad for a quick exit!

My husband still talks about the keyed deadbolt on our back door. As he tried to get out with the dogs that night, he first had to grab the key from the surface of the top stair (thank God he could still see the key lying on the staircase resting place) and then put the key into the lock. With his adrenaline running, he recalls fumbling with that single key to find the lock, get the key in right, and get it to turn. He nearly panicked. Never again! All dead bolts will have turn knobs in our home and for anti-theft considerations; we've minimized decorative door glass.

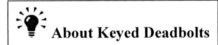 Have a Meeting Place

Many of the scariest moments for fire fighters are when they learn that Dad (or Mom) has gone back into the house because someone couldn't be accounted for, and that the one the parents went in to find was already outdoors, out of sight, and safe. Now the fire fighters have to find Mom or Dad, and pray that they can find them before disaster strikes. Identify where you'll meet. When my children were young and living with me, we picked a tree, near the sidewalk, and pledged to stand by it and not move until we knew we were each safe.

As a part of my brother's and nephews' responsibilities as fire fighters, they teach children regularly about fire safety. They bring this message home with the following story.

A few years ago, there was a house fire in a Chicago neighborhood. Two young brothers managed to safely get out of the house through different exits. (We know this because bystanders captured this activity in video footage). They didn't have a predetermined meeting place. This video footage captured the older brother anxiously looking around for his beloved younger brother and, not immediately seeing him, rushing back into the burning home, searching for the younger sibling, where he ultimately perished.

My brother tells me these children he speaks to grow very quiet at this point; and, for a moment, he lets this picture sink in. Have a meeting place. Then if someone isn't there, the *fire fighters* know what to do.

Remember to introduce your escape routes and meeting spaces to all overnight guests. It might feel silly the first few times, but you have a responsibility to those who sleep in your home. Encourage your children to ask these questions of the families they visit overnight.

In the case of our fire, we agreed before we left our bedroom to meet in the backyard. And we did. When our fire fighters arrived, they asked us first if everyone was out of the house, and how did we know this? While it felt like a crazy question at the time, I learned later that many *people remember too late, following the shock and adrenaline of the moment, that someone remains inside. In our case, we were extremely grateful that the fire happened while we were at home. A week earlier and I fear that the young couple house and dog sitting could very easily have slept through what awakened me, and by the time the smoke alarms sounded, may have ultimately perished in this fire.*

Fire Extinguishing Systems

Hand Held Fire Extinguishers

PASS. Pull, Aim, Squeeze, and Sweep. Four words to remember when you have an extinguisher in your hands—more words to live and survive by. These are the simple instructions on your home, business, or other fire extinguisher.

T🧯 PASS

P: Pull the pin, hold the extinguisher with the nozzle pointing away from you, and release the locking mechanism

A: Aim low into the fire at its base

S: Squeeze the lever slowly and firmly

S: Sweep the nozzle from side to side, low into the fire

Every hardware store and home improvement center carries home-appropriate, multi-fire-source extinguishers. Be sure to choose a multipurpose extinguisher (ABC dry-chemical); do a little research and soon you will discover that certain fires require different types of extinguishers. You may have areas of your home that require a special type of extinguisher. If you have questions, call the fire prevention or community education officer at your local fire department. They'll be happy to advise you. Whatever you buy, make sure it is large enough to put out a small fire, and light enough that most of your family members can operate it.

Be sure you read the manufacturer's directions when you purchase the equipment. The time to read is *not* when the sofa is smoldering. Generally, the four step P-A-S-S is a great, easy rule to follow. Not every fire is "extinguisher" smart though. For example, use an extinguisher only on fires confined to a waste basket or piece of furniture, in a small area, *after* everyone has exited the building, only *after* you have called the fire department, and if smoke is not filling the room. Smoke can overtake you in a matter of minutes. Seconds count, and every fire department in the country would rather have you call and then call back to say you've extinguished the fire and eliminated the danger. They'll probably still come by to make sure!

Keep an extinguisher close to the exits so that if your way is blocked, and the extinguisher can handle the job, you can clear your escape path. When using an extinguisher to hold the fire at bay during an escape, keep your back to the exit so you can easily get out if the smoke becomes too great. (You'll also be able to see family members as they race to join you).

Finally, know when to *go*! While an extinguisher can help put out a very small fire, the main element of safely surviving a fire is to *escape*.

I recommend that you get your extinguisher inspected each year, or better yet, replace them with new ones. Frequently it's less expensive to replace than to recharge. Most extinguishers also expire. There is a gauge at or near the top that will tell you if your extinguisher is in need of re-charging. When you change your smoke alarm batteries, check your extinguisher gauges. Ask your local fire department if they have a replacement, recharging, or exchange program. Some do.

Sprinkler Systems

In certain sections of the U.S., where the risk of wildfires is great and/or the supply of water is limited, building codes call for the installation of automatic sprinkler devices in residential structures. If a fire-safe home is your goal, and you are building or extensively renovating, now is the time to consider this important addition. The death rate per fire in properties with sprinklers is lower than those without by at least 57 percent. For most property uses, damage per fire is lower in homes with sprinklers by one-third to two-thirds.[8] [9]

In our case, no extinguisher or sprinkler system would likely have saved our home. The fire came from outside the house and fully engulfed the siding and soffits, penetrated the roof, and then moved through the core of the home. But just the same, we'll never build another home without a sprinkler system.

💡 Key Lessons

1. Rescue, Alert, Confine, Extinguish.

2. With a hand extinguisher, remember, Pull, Aim, Squeeze, and Sweep.

3. When the clocks change twice a year, change those smoke alarm batteries and check the gauges on your fire extinguishers.

4. Have an escape plan. Know how to get out and practice it.

5. Have a meeting place. Be sure everyone (including guests) knows where it is.

• • • • • • • • • • • • • • • • • • • •

CHAPTER THREE: GENERAL CONSTRUCTION AND RENOVATION TIPS

Building codes today are the result of research into many years of losses. Today's construction standards represent just the minimum standards for safe construction, however. There are many more steps you can take to secure your home, and frequently the additional costs for these are minimal.

Our eighty-year-old New England Colonial was "balloon" construction. Prior to the establishment of our current building standards, frame construction ran from basement to roofline without *fire-stops* between floors. In fact, the drawing that follows highlights how deadly this can be. In our case, the fire travelled up the outside of the house (the wood shingled exterior made for great kindling) into the wood soffit, over the asphalt shingled roof, down the three-story, central chimneys (and around them), and then back up the central core of the house. Today's building codes require fire-stops between floors, around chimneys, retardant flashings, etc. These fire-stops slow the spread of fire between floors, giving fire fighters a better chance of saving the structure. Balloon construction actually feeds a fire, encouraging the spread of the fire from floor to floor rapidly. Fighting this kind of fire is both dangerous for the fire fighters, and often futile. So when you remodel *any* part of that old wonderful house you love, remember to take care of what you *don't* see. Have your contractor plan fire-stops to help keep you and your home safer.

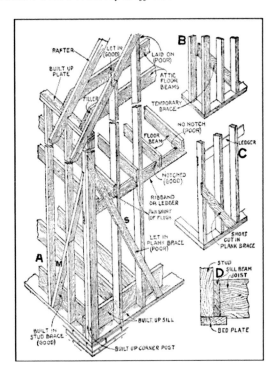

Balloon construction, courtesy of Wikipedia[10]

Remember, whether you're building or remodeling, look for these safety items along the way. Ask questions. Get educated. Don't simply trust that your builder is following the building codes or that these codes are enough. Encourage and invite inspections. You're paying for safety and security as well as the aesthetics that come with your new work. Contractors can leave things out, forget things, or overlook a potential hazard. Once the walls are covered up again, you won't know what's missing until it's too late.

🕊🏠 Exterior Home Considerations

Roofing selections are frequently dependent upon your home's location. Options include ceramic tile, slate, metal, asphalt shingles, etc. Most manufacturers can give you not only life expectancy for these options (typically twenty, thirty, forty years, or "lifetime"), but also fire ratings, resistances, fireproofing, etc. Be sure that a professional advises you about roofing materials, flashing around chimneys, vents, and skylights.

My brother just reroofed his all brick home in the Midwest with a metal fourteen-gauge material right over the existing roof, which will extend the life of his roof another one hundred years with one of the highest-rated fire-retardant materials available. Better yet, it still looks like a typical shingled roof and his one-hundred-year warranty is also transferable.

As I watched my wood shingled home with several layers of paint burn, I found what was happening twenty feet away to my neighbor's home to be amazing. Her eighty-year-old stucco home suffered minor damage as the fire department focused their efforts on saving her home immediately upon their arrival. The heat was intense, yet the stucco finish was scarcely touched at the end of the ordeal, save for a few areas of flaking paint. Conversely, her newly installed vinyl soffits and windows had melted to stages that rendered them both useless and barely recognizable. I shudder to consider the damage to her home had its siding been either wood or vinyl.

Ease of maintenance and personal aesthetics most frequently drive siding selections for a home. Clearly both wood and vinyl exteriors are far more susceptible to fire's ravages than fire-resistant brick, concrete, stucco, or metal. In certain areas of the country, these fire-resistant materials are the most economical and practical for climate-related reasons. Fire-resistant materials can slow fires that begin outside your home, such as porch fires, grass fires, and adjacent structure fires. While you may not save these homes, you may buy precious moments to escape. But remember, the wood frame beneath those vinyl or wood windows and soffits are open doors to fire from the outside. Any fire approaching from without is a reason to abandon the structure and seek shelter. Call for help, and once Mother Nature, or the fire department, have eliminated all fire danger, you can safely re-enter your home. So when you get the word to evacuate, grab that list we will create in the coming chapters, fill your carryall tote, and get out!

🐾🔥 Insulation

Usually, we check for heating and cooling efficiencies when we select our insulating materials, but don't forget to investigate combustibility, burn, and absorption rates. If this sounds extremely dull, think of it as an extra layer between an external fire and your home's contents. Not so dull now, huh? The insulation manufacturer identifies clearly on its packaging the fire rating specification for that composition. Ask your contractor to investigate the difference in cost between the ratings and make an informed decision in this area. With the right insulation, you might gain another barrier to the spread of a fire, allowing the fire fighters more time to contain the damage.

This is also a great time to make the decision about insulation not only on outside walls, but inside. Most homes have little or no insulation between rooms. Invest in extra insulation between rooms and floors and you'll sleep better (less noise), heat and cool more efficiently, and maybe even add an extra layer of fire retardation.

In many older homes, the insulation may have actually been shredded or torn paper, both in the ceiling and the walls. This was the case in our old home. Several years before my purchase, during the energy crisis of the 1970s, the home had been "improved" by drilling holes in the siding and "blowing" foam on top of this old paper insulation. Unknowingly, my walls and ceilings were a timber box, waiting for this fire.

🔥 Drywall

Ok, I know drywall is *inside* the house, but since it's in every room, we'll cover it here. Generally, most home interiors are finished with one-half-inch thickness drywall. Only garage walls and some kitchens come equipped with five-eighths-inch fire-rated drywall. For a few extra dollars, you can slow the spread of a fire from room to room or from the outside in by simply using five-eighths-inch throughout your new home or remodeled room. Better yet, go all the way to one and one-quarter-inches (two layers of five-eighths-inch) in those high-risk areas, like surrounding your kitchen, floor to ceiling, wall to wall, your laundry facilities, and any wall proximate to your attached garage, including ceilings. In addition, if you have a work or craft area where you use electrical appliances to create heat or fire, use this extra protection here. Finally, furnace rooms and home offices are high on the list of recommended areas for added protection. As a bonus, the guys who installed my drywall, or *rockers,* as they call themselves, told me with five-eighths-inch you rarely see any mudding flaws or time-related wear that you see with one-half-inch. In fact, it's what they put in their own homes. It's easier to mud and wallpaper!

Drywall Thickness and Burn time Suppression
One-half-inch = twenty minutes
Five-eighths-inch = sixty minutes
Three-quarter-inch = seventy-five minutes
One and one-quarter-inch = one hundred twenty minutes
Courtesy of Deputy Chief Christopher Millard

🐾 Electrical and Other Wiring

Electrical distribution or lighting equipment was the third leading cause of home fires and the third leading cause of fire deaths between 2002 and 2005. [11] Today's homes feature a variety of electrical service offerings, and, generally speaking, you determine your service configuration by how you live and your home's needs. Most new homes today average 200-amp service, service panels with circuit breakers, and outlets with ground faults.

Older homes, like the one I lost, are in varying stages of service upgrades to circuit breakers instead of fuse boxes, fully enclosed conduit junction boxes, and fully wrapped and insulated wire. My old home had undergone that full upgrade at some point, except, it seems, for the outdoor porch. Homes older than fifty years may have knob and tube wiring—where the bare copper wire that conducts the current wraps around a ceramic knob and joins another bare copper conduit. This type of wiring is *always* "hot" or "live" even when the switch is in the "off" position.

In my case, this is the system that was present between my living room wall switch and the ceiling fan suspended from the outside porch, directly below my master bedroom. It seems that somehow, something caused those live wires to spark and ignite the wood supports and/or the two-inch, wooden, tongue-in-groove ceiling on that porch that spring evening.

I suppose the electrician that put the fan in for me thirteen years prior might have known knob and tube wiring was what was present; and, while it is really a very efficient way to conduct electricity, I can't look back and not ask *was it safe?* As far as I'm concerned, I'd never sleep in a room again if I knew any part of the house still had knob and tube wiring.

If you are building, or remodeling, talk to your licensed master electrician and account for the amount and type of service that will meet your needs. Look at your rooms and think about not only your everyday needs, but also special or occasional uses. Where will you put your Christmas tree? How about special occasion lighting? Will you have enough outlets in the right locations to accommodate your needs? Also, remember to be sure to maintain a three foot clearance around your electrical panel and keep that area clear of all combustible materials.

In our new home, we put outlets everywhere. My husband and I really enjoy decorating for the holidays, so we included grounded outlets (on a wall switch, with an energy saving timer) at each corner of our roof line outside the home, to allow for hanging icicle lights. We also put outlets under every window sill inside our home for those electric candles that sit on the sill. That way, when the lights go up, there are no extension cords, no multiple outlet adapters, and no additional stress on our electrical system. The difference? Well, I recall one Christmas, the year before the fire in fact,

23

when my son-in-law and his friends helped me install roof line lights, an extensive outdoor display with trees and reindeer in various poses, over twenty indoor window lights, and a huge live tree. Dusk finally arrived and we had all gathered to turn on the lights (they all plugged into about four outlets). The lights came on dramatically to the ahhhhhs of the crew and then proceeded to take out the three circuits into which I had plugged the connectors. We spent about a week reconfiguring, adding more extension cords, etc., until we had the load balanced into a combination that wouldn't overload the circuits. I should have known better, but didn't.

Everything You Ever Wanted to Know About Electric Circuit Interrupters[12]

AFCIs (arc-fault circuit-interrupters)

When an electrical switch is opened or closed, an arc, or discharge of electricity across a circuit, occurs. Unintentional arcs can occur at loose connections or where wear and tear have damaged the wires or cords. Such arcs can lead to high temperatures and sparking, possibly igniting combustibles. Designed to discriminate between unintended arcing and the type of arcing that occurs when a operating a switch, AFCIs (arc-fault circuit-interrupters) protect against fire by continuously monitoring the electrical current in a circuit and shutting off the circuit when unintended arcing occurs.

GFCIs (ground-fault circuit-interrupters)

A ground-fault is an unintentional electrical path between a source of electrical current and a grounded surface. Electrical shock can occur if a person comes into contact with an energized part. GFCIs (ground-fault circuit-interrupters) can greatly reduce the risk of shock by immediately shutting off an electrical circuit when that circuit represents a shock hazard (i.e., a person comes in contact with a faulty appliance together with a grounded surface). An electrician can install GFCIs in a circuit breaker panel board or directly in a receptacle outlet.

• The *National Electrical Code®* *(NEC)* requires **AFCI** installation in bedrooms of new residential construction (effective as of January 1, 2002). The NEC selected bedrooms as the first area in which to implement this requirement because of a history of fires there.

• The *NEC* requires **GFCI** installation for receptacles in kitchens, bathrooms, outdoor areas, basements and garages in new residential construction because of a history of shock hazards in these areas.

Source: the National Fire Prevention Association's website: http://www.nfpa.org/research/NFPAfactsheets

💡 How a Fire Fighter Buys a Home

—-contributed by Deputy Chief, Chris Millard, Byron Fire Protection District, Byron, Illinois

When most people look for a home or home site, they consider tax rates, school districts, views, location to work, play, recreation areas, etc. But how many people pay a visit to their local fire, police, and EMS offices? How many people check to find the location of fire hydrants and evaluate the distance to their home? Average response times for fire or EMS teams? Minutes to the nearest fire or police station? Is it a volunteer or paid on call or full time staff on these critical teams? What do you know about the teams that your home, your family, and your lives depend upon?

Is the EMS or ambulance/rescue team basic, life support, or advanced? How far do you have to travel from your home to the nearest hospital? Will it take a crew five, ten, or even fifteen minutes to get to you? The time to learn about these things is not when you are waiting to hear the approaching siren.

Pay a visit to these community units before you buy. At the fire station, take the time to meet the chief and the staff officers. They'll tell you what they know about the area you're considering. They'll show you their statistics and their fire response equipment. It just might make a difference to you to learn whether the newest equipment was purchased in 1962 or 2007. Is the department or district adequately funded to take care of its residents? Are these teams prepared for a local disaster? Do they have formal plans?

Remember, in an emergency, the responding agency will likely only respond within their normal capacity. Know what this is. A remote home site that lies five to ten miles out of town, up a two-mile private lane with low hanging trees, branches, and wires can cost you precious time in an emergency. Make sure those sharp turns, narrow lanes, narrow decorative gates, etc., don't keep a fire truck and crew from accessing your home!

At a minimum, your visit introduces you to some great people who will be your new neighbors. You get to know them in advance of any need, in the worst case scenario, and perhaps get to start a new friendship.

Think Safe—Be Safe,

Deputy Chief, Christopher R. Millard
Byron Fire Protection District, Byron, IL

Key Lessons:

1. Whether building or remodeling, make fire smart selections in your building materials.

2. Roofing shingles, insulation, exterior finishes, and drywall choices can all deter or delay a fire's progress.

3. Electrical distribution equipment and distribution disregard are historically major causes of home fires.

4. Consider how you use your home and consult your builder or electrician for advice when building or remodeling.

5. Before you buy or build, make a stop at the local EMS offices and meet/talk to the experts.

• • • • • • • • • • • • • • • • • • • •

CHAPTER FOUR: THE KITCHEN

Fire in one- and two-family dwellings most often originates in the kitchen (32 percent) and more than half (62 percent) of all apartment fires start in the kitchen! As you have probably guessed, cooking equipment was the leading source of these kitchen fires.[13] And, as you probably further suspected, human error was the single largest cause. Based upon 2002–05 statistics, it looks like this:

- 151,500 home structure fires

- 4,800 injuries

- 440 deaths

- $823 million in direct property damage. [14]

BAD NEWS: most likely place for a fire
Kitchen fires led the pack as the origin of most home fires.
GOOD NEWS: not as deadly as elsewhere
Kitchen fires ranked third, in area of origin, for home fires that resulted in death.

⛽💡 Kitchen Safety Tips[15]

⛽ If you have a fire, call the fire department immediately. Get help on its way, then take these actions.

- *Never, never, never* leave cooking unattended: not while you leave the room for just a second, or run to the corner store—never, never, never. Turn it off until you are there to monitor.

- Use only cooking equipment tested and approved by a recognized testing facility.

- Keep cooking areas and surfaces free of combustibles, like pot holders, towels, rags, drapes, food packaging, oils, etc. Take that lovely, decorative towel *off* the oven door handle. Don't store items on the stove or in the oven. Use your cupboards for this, not your heating appliances.

- Make a three foot kid/pet-free zone around all cooking surfaces, indoors and out.

- Always turn pot handles inward so you or a child can't bump, or unintentionally pull, the pan from the heating surfaces.

⛽ Keep a pot holder, oven mitt, and pot lid handy in the event of trouble. *If a grease fire starts in a pan, put the mitt on your hand and immediately put the lid on the pot to smother the fire—then turn off the burner. Do not remove the pot from the stove or the lid from the pot until the pan is cool.*

⛽ If you have an oven fire, *keep the door closed*, turn the oven off, and keep the door closed until the fire self extinguishes. Opening the door will only feed the fire and may cause it to spread, both to your kitchen and your clothing. Then when the fire is out, make sure you know why it started. If your oven is soiled, clean it manually so that you don't risk further fire by using the auto clean feature. If you are not sure why the fire started, call your appliance repair specialist.

⛽ In the event of a microwave fire, carefully unplug the device (cover your hand as the cord could be hot as well) and immediately call the fire department. Don't mess with this appliance. *Do not use* this microwave again, ever. Have it serviced by a certified repair facility or replace it.

▌ Similarly, with any other electrical kitchen appliance that smokes, sparks, or appears to be on fire, turn it off, and unplug it immediately. Call the fire department if there is any sign of actual fire, and when the appliance is cool enough to touch, *throw it away*! It's time for a new toaster, toaster oven, coffee pot, mixer, blender, food processor, can opener, knife sharpener, etc. (It's a perfect excuse to get the newest gadget in the designer color you've been coveting!)

▌ Fashion aside, do not cook while wearing flowing or loose clothing, sleeves that dangle, or scarves that could easily catch fire if they brush a burner or open flame. Do not wear bell sleeves, flowing bathrobes, caftans, or shawls while you are at the stove, grill, or oven.

▌ Similarly, tie back those lovely long locks and keep them out of both the fire and the soup!

▌ If you have concerns over children or an elderly family member reaching/using the stove, purchase cook tops with knobs that are either out of reach or removable. Removing and hiding these knobs can also discourage any lousy or messy cooks in the household!

▌ Keep those appliance cords neatly wound behind the appliance, unplugged when not in use (except the refrigerator, of course), and secured with one of the thousands of twisty ties you have stashed in the junk drawer. Even better, when possible, store those unplugged appliances and keep them out of harm's way. Just be sure the appliances used for heating—like toaster, toaster oven, or electric coffee pot—are cool completely before storing.

▌ *Never* use your stove or oven to heat the room or your home. CO (carbon monoxide) and fire are both life-risking possibilities. If your home is without heat, stay with a family member, friend, neighbor, or call a local service organization for a shelter that can house you until you have your situation remedied.

If you have a grease fire:

DO

1. Put a mitt on your hand and immediately put the lid on the pot.

2. Turn off the burner.

3. Step away from the stove.

DO NOT

1. Remove the lid from the pot until the pan and its contents are cool to the touch.

2. Carry the pan outdoors.

3. Use water on a grease fire.

4. Discharge a fire extinguisher on a pan of burning grease, unless you know you have the right type of extinguisher, and you have received training in its use.

Any of these actions can actually cause the fire to spread or splatter creating a greater problem and/or causing you serious injuries. [16]

 Water

Fire is not the only preventable disaster that can strike your home. Fire's foe, water, can do just as much damage. Sinks, leaking toilet tanks, improper shut off/flow valves, refrigerator water lines, washing machine hoses, and dishwashers can all be the source of the second home destroyer: water (a frequent partner with smoke and fire). Be sure you have leaks repaired by a licensed plumber. A little water can eventually fill a room, rot a floor, and generally cause mold and other menaces that can actually compromise the integrity of your structure. [17]

> *Did you know?*
> One home with three faucets dripping at the rate of sixty drips per minute creates a water loss of twenty-two gallons per day. Now consider the impact if any of those dripping faucets or sources don't have a drain.

 # Fire Discouraging Surfaces and Finishes

Walls

As described in chapter three, the walls surrounding your stove and the kitchen ceiling are a must for installing five-eighths-inch drywall, according to most current building codes. But since we know this area to be the most frequent source of home fires, I plan to use five-eighths-inch to surround my entire kitchen. Actually, knowing what we know now, we'll likely double this for these areas to one and one-quarter-inch thickness. This way, I'll buy more time for extinguishing the fire, and possibly minimize my losses in other rooms of the house should I ever have a kitchen fire.

Keep loose wallpaper replaced or repaired. Loose wallpaper can catch fire rapidly if exposed to an open flame. Be sure the wall behind your stove or cook top has added protection, like tile or metal, and keep it free of grease and dust. Remove decorative clutter, like pot holders, curtains, drapes, aprons, macramé, and spices. Any of these things near an open flame, like your gas stove, or a very hot surface, like your electric stove, can fuel a fire.

Floors

Natural surfaces, such as stone and ceramic, are more resistant to fire conduction than wood, vinyl, or carpet. If your sub-floor and supporting joists are wood, however, then fire from below will still spread to your kitchen. Only concrete and dirt make your floor truly fire safe. Matches, lit cigarettes, and burning candles are the greatest risk to most floor surfaces. Use caution around carpets and area rugs when using any of these items.

Counters

Stone, such as granite, marble, and the newer stone composites, are generally great for preventing a fire that might originate on a countertop. Remember, though, your countertop is usually supported by wood cabinetry; and, fire loves wood. Never leave a candle burning or a lit cigarette unattended in *any* room, on any surface. Also, pay attention to those appliances on the counter top. Be sure to replace any frayed wiring with new; or, simply toss the appliance and buy a new one. Don't overload those counter outlets, and only use under cabinet lighting designed specifically for this use.

Kitchen budgets vary widely. Work within your budget and where you have options, understand not only the beauty and functionality of the choices you make, but also their safety.

💡 Protecting Kitchen Items

I promised that as we toured the home, I'd discuss ways to protect your important items from harm if/when the unthinkable happens.

Don't overlook taking photos of the inventory in your kitchen. As you walk through and take photographs, open the cupboards, drawers, etc. If you ever have to replace the contents of a room and document what you possessed at the time of a loss, a picture is not only worth a thousand words, it can be worth thousands of dollars.

Many people do their home bookkeeping in their kitchen and store many receipts, records, and papers in a kitchen file or desk. I suggest that you invest in a small fire-safe file cabinet or small file-sized, water-tight container in which to store these current items. This will buy you a few hours to get your documents out before fire will destroy the safe. I keep receipts for everything valued in excess of $100, filed in an envelope by room of location, and then tucked into these water-tight files. This, coupled with my photos, is all the documentation I will need if I ever have another loss. Finally, zippered plastic storage bags will also keep water and smoke/soot from damaging important papers.

As suggested earlier, carry a pad of paper with you (or this book, turned to the last page in this chapter) and consider the things you'd grab from your kitchen if you had five to ten minutes warning to get out.

💡 In addition, you might consider taking the following preservation measures:

1. Use zipper-equipped, plastic storage bags or sealed, plastic containers to store the cloth napkins, tablecloths, and dish towels that your grandmother embroidered and handed down to you. This will protect them from both smoke and water stains that might occur. It may even slow the effects of aging on these articles.

2. Similarly, instead of stacking cookbooks in a closed cupboard, consider putting these books in a plastic tub, organized and labeled in such a way as to easily locate and store them. This will protect your prized treasures from grease, smoke, water, and dust—all things that age and ruin these pricey investments. If you want to keep your cookbooks handy in a cupboard, try putting each one in its own zippered,

plastic, storage bag. Even though the fire in my home never reached my kitchen, I lost my entire collection of cookbooks (well over fifty in number) to smoke and water damage. Had I stored them in this fashion, I'd still have them today.

3. Store fine china and other collectibles not on display in plastic storage tubs, covered securely. If the kitchen, dining room, or storage area are flooded, or have smoke and water damage from a fire elsewhere in the home, your china will now float and the smoke will not penetrate its delicate composition. Smoke and soot will bake into china, glass, and ceramic when temperatures from a fire reach them. In a matter of minutes, the composition of these items is forever changed. Let that tub absorb the soot and smoke. Tossing it will be less painful than tossing those heirlooms.

You see, as I went room to room after my fire, I thought, ok, my dining room and kitchen had no actual fire damage, and the ceiling and walls didn't collapse in and break everything, so maybe my dishes and glassware could just be cleaned up. Ha! The actual composition of these items had changed. The intense heat allowed the smoke to infiltrate and destroy the glass, penetrate all fabrics, and then the water set the damage permanently. Yet, in the cellar, a floor away, the smoke and water had not penetrated those rubber tubs with lids holding my Christmas decorations.

The kitchen, after the fire.

Remember that fire destroys all it touches and typically creates enough heat to destroy things a floor or two rooms away. Smoke and water typically only destroy what they penetrate. By adding another layer to penetrate, you add protection that just might save your grandmother's precious hand-me-down.

 # Key Lessons:

1. Never leave items cooking unattended.

2. Keep fabrics and combustibles away from the stove and oven.

3. Don't store groceries, dishes, or other items in your oven.

4. If you have a stove top fire in a pan, put a lid on the pan and turn off the stove. Do not carry this pan outside or to the sink. Do not remove the lid until the pan is cool.

5. If you have an oven fire, turn it off and leave the door to the oven closed.

6. Get all water leaks repaired.

7. Consider using rubber tubs with lids, or zippered, plastic bags in which to store infrequently used kitchen treasures.

Stow, Grab & Go List: Kitchen

CHAPTER FIVE: THE DINING ROOM

The dining room is not a frequent source of home fires, but this is a great place to talk about a few things that can crop up in here, your living room, or bedroom.

Candles

The biggest culprits in starting fires in the dining room are candles. Candles plus tablecloths, drapes, napkins, and wood equal fire. *Never* leave candles burning in *any* room while you adjourn to a different room. Vigilance is a must.

NFPA data shows that home fires involving candles peak on Christmas Day, New Year's Day, and Christmas Eve. Candle fires represent about 10 percent of the home structure fires that occur on those days. In 2005 alone, candles, resulting in 150 civilian deaths, 1,270 civilian injuries, and an estimated direct property loss of $539 Million, started 15,600 home fires.[18]

How does a little fire become so dangerous? NFPA reports that two out of ten times people leave these fragrant, lovely items unattended. We set the table, light the candles, put the centerpiece on the table, and then go back to the kitchen to finish preparing the meal; or, maybe we finish our dinner, grab our beverage, and adjourn to the den—each thinking the other has attended to the candles. Even worse, we forget about the candle in the bath/bedroom as we go to sleep. About 55 percent of candle related fires are the direct result of people placing candles too near a combustible like a dried centerpiece, loose billowy curtains, etc. Finally, be attentive to children drawn to the magic of that little flame. Too many young lives are lost each year to children playing with fire.[19]

🔥 Candle Safety

1. Keep candles at least 12 inches from anything that can burn.
2. Use sturdy, safe candleholders.
3. Never leave a burning candle unattended. Extinguish candles when you leave a room.
4. Be careful not to splatter wax when extinguishing a candle.
5. Avoid using candles in bedrooms and sleeping areas.
6. Always use a flashlight, not a candle, for emergency lighting.
7. Consider using battery-operated flameless candles.[20]

🔥 Light Fixtures/Chandeliers

Improperly wired light fixtures and chandeliers, or fixtures with combustible fabrics and decorations affixed to the same, are more culprits for starting fires, not only in the dining room but other rooms as well.

I've already confessed to my passion for Christmas lights. Well, I actually go pretty crazy at other times as well. Have you ever bought that fake spider webbing and then draped it from chandelier to side wall or light fixture for an eerie Halloween effect? I certainly have. Since the fire, I've started to read those packages a bit more closely and have learned that few, if any, of these decorative materials are fire-resistant. How many of us have actually scorched a finger or lampshade on a hot light bulb? Imagine this webbing or a piece of fabric on one of those hot bulbs! It wouldn't take much time at all to start a fire.

It's important to read the manufacturers' suggested wattage capacity for light fixtures. Select the lowest wattage appropriate; and, while you are at it, buy some of the new, low wattage, energy efficient, good-for-the-environment, fluorescent bulbs. They will help save the earth, and they burn *cooler* than all other options! At a minimum, replace your bulbs today in the closet, attic, and cupboards with these cool, efficient alternatives.

Have you ever removed a burned out bulb in a lamp and then taken a while to replace it? Remember that this receptacle is a live source of electrical current. Dust can accumulate in these empty receptacles and actually become a source of trouble. With so many switches on the wall, and habits of turning on a lamp, it is easy enough to forget there is no bulb in that lamp, and before you know it, you have a smoking lamp. Keep a supply of bulbs for every fixture and replace spent bulbs with new ones immediately; and when you dust your lovely dining room table, dust that chandelier!

Protecting Your Finery

This is a great place to use those oversized plastic zippered bags to seal and store fine linens that you have tucked away in the side board or side table drawers. Consider placing your expensive china place settings and serving pieces in dust protectors and *then* into plastic tubs with sealed lids. You've just made these heirloom pieces less penetrable to smoke and water. I like to display these pretty dishes, so I put out one place setting in my glass bureau, and put the rest in these tubs and store them away. That way, the next time I have a loss, I will only have to replace one place setting instead of all twelve. As a bonus, I don't have to dust the other eleven place settings when I go to set the table.

As for glassware, I discovered that leaded crystal held up to the heat, smoke, and water considerably better than non-leaded glass and crystal. In fact, we had received matching wedding gifts of heavy Waterford crystal goblets, a wine bottle holder, and a vase. The combination of these items still sitting in their boxes, coupled with their lead composition, allowed these treasures to be among the very few items surviving our fire.

The damage in our dining room—and the "fire" didn't reach this area

 Key Lessons

1. Candles require constant attention and special precautions.

2. Light fixtures and chandeliers require cleaning and caution. Keep fabrics away from hot bulbs and replace spent bulbs immediately with bulbs that meet manufacturers recommended wattages.

3. Be kind to the environment and replace your bulbs with cooler, energy efficient, fluorescent bulbs.

4. Protect china, crystal, and linens by storing them in smoke and water resistant materials.

Stow, Grab & Go List: Dining Room

_____

_____

_____

_____

_____

_____

_____

_____

_____

_____

_____

_____

_____

_____

_____

_____

_____

_____

_____

_____

_____

_____

_____

_____

_____

_____

CHAPTER SIX: LIVING ROOMS, FAMILY ROOMS, AND DENS

In considering the origins of home fires within these areas, our worst enemy seems to be ourselves. Careless smoking, unattended candles or lanterns, room or area heaters, too many or worn extension cords, frayed lamp wires, overloaded outlets, unattended fireplaces, neglected chimneys, overfed fires in wood burning fireplaces, and insufficient or absent fireplace screens/doors most frequently start the fires in the rooms in which we relax. Most of these fires are very preventable.

Careless Use of Tobacco Products

Careless use of tobacco products is the leading cause of *death*. Yes, in addition to the implications to your lungs and other organs from the number one cause of cancer, fully 25 percent of all people who die in a house fire do so because someone was smoking in a chair, sofa, or bed.[21] If you must smoke and you are fatigued, *stand up and go outside*!

Overflowing ashtrays, dumping ashtrays' contents into a trash receptacle while still hot, or overturning ashtrays are frequent sources of smoking-related fires.

 **Smoking Apparatus Advice**

- Don't smoke.

- Extinguish all smoking materials in heavy ash trays, clean and of a non-combustible material. *Do not* throw your lit cigarettes out of a car, home window, or door. As Smokey the Bear has taught us, *only you can prevent a forest fire!*

- Wet, with water, all ashes before discarding the same into a trash container.

- Never go to bed with a cigarette. *Never.* There is *no* safe way to smoke and lie down. *None. Period.*

Courtesy of Deputy Chief C. R. Millard, who has carried out enough victims from a burning chair and bed to be an expert!

Hurricane Lanterns

We learned in the last chapter about the risks of candles. Lit hurricane lanterns can be equally dangerous, as are lamps placed on tables that are too small or wobbly. Place your table lamp on a surface that is at least one and one-half times the circumference of the lamp's shade.

Floor Lamps

Floor lamps are frequently great additions to these rooms designed for relaxation, but avoid purchasing lamps whose bases are too small, or have extremely hot light sources. Don't place lamps too close to drapery, other combustible fabrics, or in areas where pets or children might easily tip them over.

Extension Cords, Frayed Wires, and Overloaded Outlets

Extension cords, frayed wires, and overloaded outlets can also be a source of fire danger. Cords and plugs caused 12 percent of all home electrical distribution fires and 39 percent of related deaths. [22] Have you ever, like me, run an extension cord under an area rug, across the room, to reach a lamp that didn't have an outlet? Well, imagine what will happen if you have an arc or spark under that rug? Foot traffic can cause wear in the cord itself, or it can loosen the plug's connection to the extension cord. This can cause a smoky, smoldering fire.

 **Safety Tips[23]**

- Replace or repair loose or frayed cords on all electrical devices, including lamps. Do not wrap black electrical tape—or any other type of tape—around the connection. Have a professional electrician or appliance repair person repair the item.

- Avoid running extension cords across doorways or under carpets and rugs.

- In homes with small children, unused electrical outlets and extension cord receptacles should have plastic safety caps. You can buy these in larger toy stores, hardware stores, home improvement centers, and electrical supply houses.

- Consider having additional circuits or outlets added by a qualified electrician so you do not have to use extension cords.

- Follow the manufacturer's instructions for plugging an appliance into a receptacle outlet.

- Place lamps on level surfaces, away from things that can burn and use bulbs that match the lamp's recommended wattage.

- Avoid overloading outlets. Plug only one high-wattage appliance into a receptacle outlet at a time (i.e., don't plug the refrigerator and microwave into the same outlet).

- If outlets or plugs feel warm, shut off the circuit and have them inspected by a licensed electrician.

- When possible, avoid the use of "cube taps" and other devices that allow the connection of multiple appliances into a single receptacle.

 **Fireplaces**

Let me begin with this observation: the quickest way to overcome a desire for a wood burning fireplace is to watch your home burn. I love to curl up in front of a nice fireplace on a cold evening and watch a licking fire warm my feet, yet somehow the smell and sounds of that fire haunt me. Our new home has two gas fireplaces. That's *our* new standard.

Wood burning fireplaces can be a dangerous source of home fires if not properly attended. Here are some simple safe practices that might allow you to enjoy this home feature:

1. Never leave your fire and hot embers to go to bed or leave the house. One popping ember is all it takes to bring down your home. Be sure you have, and use, a fire screen that completely covers your fireplace opening; or, even better, have a fire-rated, tempered glass door enclosure that you can secure to snuff out those last embers safely.

2. Never burn paper, trash, or other items in your fireplaces. These decorative home accents, designed for the safe burning only of approved starter and wood products, become hazardous when you try to burn items not intended by the manufacturer for this fixture. Burning other items in a fireplace can lead to a fire you cannot control, or cause a rapid accumulation of chemicals on the inside of your chimney that can damage or narrow the chimney flue. Never use a liquid combustible like gasoline, kerosene, or charcoal lighter fluid to start an indoor fire in your fireplace. These liquids can quickly cause a fire to burn out of control, shoot into the room, or onto your clothing. In addition, the fumes from fires like these can also be life threatening.

3. Never burn anything in a gas fireplace. Once you convert a fireplace to gas by the installation of a gas pipe and log, you should exclusively use that fireplace as a gas fireplace.

4. Building codes in many areas today require, or encourage, permanently open dampers for all gas fireplaces and dampers that manually open and close for all wood burning fireplaces.

5. Never close a damper until the last ember has cooled. The smallest hot ember in a fireplace can fill a room with smoke and carbon monoxide in a matter of minutes.

6. Be sure to vent and clean all fireplaces according to manufacturer's instructions. Have your chimneys cleaned by a professional at least every five to seven years. Failure to do so can result in a chimney fire. If you ever notice flames coming from the top of a chimney, call the fire department immediately. This could be a chimney fire that can easily spread to the roofing or structure.

7. Never build a fire so large in your fireplace that any portion of the materials or flames extends beyond any part of the fireplace opening. The safest practice is to keep the amount of wood to half the width and a quarter of the height of your opening, and the flames to not more than two-thirds of the height of the opening.

8. Don't put carpet or area rugs on or near your hearth. Use fire-retardant materials, like marble, brick, granite, or ceramic to create at least a twenty-four inch hearth in front of the full width of your fireplace.

9. Never dispose of fireplace embers—hot, warm, or cool—into a trash receptacle not specifically designed for the same. Don't store an ash receptacle near any building structure. I watched an acquaintance lose his multi-million dollar contemporary home in the woods (and all of his amazing collectibles) to a fire that was the result of carelessly discarding fireplace embers in a plastic trash can housed in the attached garage. Fortunately, the fire injured no one, but the home and its contents were a total loss. This loss was so very preventable.

Televisions/Receivers/Stereos/ Recording Devices/ Cable Connections

As our TV's get fancier and their attachments more plentiful, it is important to monitor the outlets we use, the connections we make, and the frequency with which we clean and check the same. Some of these appliances generate a significant amount of heat while in operation. Be sure each appliance is clean, free of dust, and properly ventilated. Avoid placing combustibles, like paper and cellophane, around or near these items.

Be sure a licensed professional installs your home's phone and cable. Never staple these cords to your walls or floors. These wires carry electrical signals and arcing is a serious possibility. If you are securing this cabling to the exterior of your walls, affix the appropriate securing mechanism first, then feed the wire through.

Christmas Trees, Wreathes and Roping

I've mentioned my passion for all things Christmas once or twice already; and my favorite thing is to hang live wreaths (with lights of course) on the larger windows or over the fireplace. I also like to place live roping and fresh greens on the fireplace mantles. I just love the smell of evergreens. Well, one hot ember popping up from the fireplace onto the greens may result in a serious fire, quickly dampening any holiday and probably destroy the room you are in.

Candles, arcing lights (too many connections, missing or broken bulbs), and careless embers can also ignite these fresh, drying branches in seconds. The same risks exist with your tree.

Holiday Lighting and Tree Safety Tips[24]

1. When decorating your tree, always use lights listed by a testing laboratory. Manufacturers design some lights for indoor or outdoor use, but not both. Larger tree lights should also have some type of reflector rather than a bare bulb.

2. Follow the manufacturer's instructions on how to use tree lights. Do not use any string of lights with worn, frayed, or broken cords or loose bulb connections. Connect no more than three strands of push-in bulbs and a maximum of fifty bulbs for screw-in bulbs.

3. Bring outdoor electrical lights inside after the holidays to prevent hazards and extend their life.

4. Always unplug Christmas tree lights before leaving home or going to sleep. *(I actually keep mine on a timer to turn them off so I don't forget.)*

5. Never use lit candles to decorate a tree, and be careful placing candles among greens and other decorations on your mantle, table, or other surface.

6. Try to keep live trees as moist as possible by giving them plenty of water. Do not purchase a tree that is dry or dropping needles.

7. Choose a sturdy tree stand designed not to tip over.

8. Be sure to purchase artificial trees labeled as fire retardant.

9. Children are fascinated with Christmas trees (of course!). Watch them closely and do not let them play with the wiring or lights.

10. Make sure the tree is at least three feet from any heat source and try to position it near the outlet, so that cords are not running long distances. *Use caution so as not to place the tree in a location that may block an exit.*

11. Safely dispose of the tree when it begins dropping needles. Dried out trees and greens are highly flammable, and should neither be left in

a house, in a garage, nor placed up against the house. Never cut up the tree and burn it in a fireplace. Firs, evergreen branches, and their needles emit a tar-like substance that is harmful to your fireplace and chimney.

🔥 Flooring, Fabrics & Finishes

Carpet and area rugs are popular choices for this part of our home. Be sure to seek fire-retardant options when selecting your carpet. The higher the rating, the longer you have to discover the fire before it consumes the house.

Keep fabric furnishings like drapes, blankets, etc., clear of electrical outlets and other heat sources. Use caution when placing candles and decorative lighting in your home so that your fabrics remain clear of contact.

If you select fabric or paper wall coverings, keep open flames away from the walls. Avoid items like wall mounted lanterns and candles. Be sure these finishes remain securely affixed to the walls. These fabrics and paper dry out with age and become highly flammable.

All that remained of our living room. The fire started
just outside the wall you see on the right.

Different agencies rate furniture, its fabrics, and cushions to indicate whether they have met certain standards for flammability, combustibility, burn times, and melting factors. California led the way in this area with the formation of the Bureau of Home furnishings in 1972. This bureau published standards as early as 1984, and has come to publish and republish standards through its California Technical Bulletins. California Technical

Bulletin (CAL) 116 (1980) is a standard that addresses the *Requirements, Test Procedures, and Apparatus for Testing the Flame Retardance of Upholstered Furniture*. CAL 117 (1980) is a standard that addresses the *Requirements, Test Procedures, and Apparatus for Testing the Flame Retardance of Resilient Filling Materials Used in Upholstered Furniture*, and CAL 133 (1984/1991) is a standard for the *Flammability Test Procedures for Seating Furniture in Use in Public Occupancies*. Similarly, Underwriters Laboratory has a standard for flammability of plastic materials (UL94).

Together, furniture manufacturers and material manufacturers around the country are now applying these standards. Several states have adopted these standards for furniture in public places, and if you want to minimize your risk, you might begin looking at labels or ordering custom fabrics and foams that meet or exceed these standards. [25] For example, to pass CAL 133, a manufacturer must design a piece of furniture with a combination of materials including fabric, cushioning material, and fire blocker, such as DuPont's Kevlar®, that ensures overall safety.[26]

 **Prevention Step—Photo Preservation**

Sometime after dawn, the fire incident commander came up to me and said, "We have the fire contained, for now, and we hope to have it out within the next hour or so. I can send one man in safely. Is there anything you want to save?" Well, I was in shock. I couldn't think. I said, "Can he return to the second floor bedroom and get my wedding rings and glasses?" Now, that part of the house is where the fire had been the hottest. There was neither much of a wall on that side of the house nor any roof, and yet I held out hope that somehow the marble topped night stand, next to the bed where we had been sleeping, would still be safely guarding my beautiful ring and much needed eyewear! (see the photo that follows)

This is the second floor bedroom where we slept. The arrow is pointing to the window which we looked out of to discover the fire. The porch where the fire started is no longer visible.

Moments later, that firefighter, who went in to assess the safety of entry as his primary purpose for going in, now stood in front of me. He reached into his pocket and produced my rings and glasses. I was so lucky— and overwhelmed. (I learned later that this firefighter burned his hand retrieving these items for me.)

The fire chief then suggested I think real hard. Did I have one central place where I stored family photos, memory books, or other valuable items? I was so glad he asked me. These had not yet occurred to me. In fact, I did have a central location for most of my cherished photos. They were in a cabinet in my lower level family room where there had been no fire, but by this time, nearly a foot of water filled the area and smoke had damaged everything in its wake. Moments later, this same firefighter emerged with a garbage bag, filled with about a dozen wet, sooty, photo albums. That's when my loving friends dug in. They each took an album home; and, by carefully disassembling these treasures, removing the delicately captured moments in my life, and through gingerly cleaning, drying, and sorting the photos, these friends were able to save a collection of personal memories. I was so lucky. These friends presented the restored photos to me in the plastic tubs they remain in today.

I did, however, lose two wedding albums (my new one and my daughter's) that had been on my coffee table, as well as every photo hanging on any wall or otherwise displayed framed. As you might guess, many of these were the only existing copy of that photo.

Today, I not only have a duplicate photo of every framed or displayed photo, but I also have a digital copy stored both on my computer and on a portable hard drive which I keep tucked into a fire-rated six-hour safe. Don't forget to include those expensive professional frames in your inventory of assets. Take a photo and put it with the receipts. I now store all of my unframed photos by subject matter in a plastic, sealed tub, inside yet another plastic tub, holding multiple smaller tubs. Now, the photos won't get wet, they won't absorb smoke, and with two layers of protection, they *may* not even melt. When I want to share these memories with others, I just pull out my tubs. I admit, we do briefly laugh about this not-so-glamorous way of storing photos; but, knowing how much we have learned since that fateful fire, I can live with less glamour.

 **Key Lessons**

1. Don't smoke lying down, or while fatigued in a chair.

2. Place table lamps and floor lamps securely where they won't fall, tip over, or touch fabrics.

3. Use extension cords and outlet extenders with caution.

4. A professional should replace frayed cords or faulty appliance wires immediately.

5. Avoid overloading outlets.

6. Use caution around fireplaces. Clean and maintain according to manufacturer's instructions.

7. Maintain your chimneys.

8. Use caution with Christmas and holiday lighting and decorations.

9. Buy fire-rated fabrics and furnishings.

10. Store your photos digitally and in print. Store prints in rubber or plastic lidded tubs, in dry and safe areas.

Stow, Grab & Go List: Living Room, Family Room, Den

CHAPTER SEVEN: THE HOME OFFICE OR LIBRARY

While neither a frequent source of a home fire, nor the most likely place to perish in a fire, the home office and home library *can* be the source of the *greatest* loss. This is where we store valuable records, expensive books, and our very expensive home computers and related peripherals.

For prevention, reread the sections on wiring, dust collection, lighting, extension cords, frayed cords, and electrical distribution (chapter 6). Many of us purchase six-outlet surge protectors for our home computer gadgets; frequently putting two of these in the same outlet nearest the computer desk. Be aware of the risks associated with doing this. It's bad for the performance of this expensive equipment, and you run the risk of overloading or overheating these circuits.

Many computer desks come today with storage nooks and crannies for all your great peripherals. However, I have found that many fail to have adequate ventilation for these same features. Be sure to remove the backs to these desks and install a small, battery-operated fan to keep the air around this equipment cool. Your computer will work better, last longer, and not become a fire risk.

Power this equipment down at night or when you'll be away from home. Why run the risk of having it overheat or start a fire. This practice will also extend the life of much of the equipment and may save yours!

As for the library and that wonderful collection of books, CDs, and DVDs, it's hard to find a way to display and use these items and still keep them out of harm's way. Be aware of what shares these shelves. Resist placing candles and other flammables near these surfaces.

I've created a system using an Excel spreadsheet to catalogue by genre all music (CDs) and movies (DVDs). Now, when we add a new one to our collection, I add it to the list. I keep a copy of it with my other inventory documents. If I ever have another loss, I have a detailed record of what we own. (If you'd like a copy of these Excel spreadsheets, make a request on the website http://www.isurvivedahousefire.com)

Protecting Your Home Office Items

I lost hundreds of books that were stored in my basement on makeshift bookshelves. I regret not having these books (many of which were old college textbooks or already-read novels) packed away in plastic-lidded storage tubs. My books were lost to the water that fell those three stories through my house. Wet and dirty, they were beyond salvage.

Today, I have roughly one hundred titles in my office/library because I reference them frequently in my work; and the remainder of my infrequently consulted volumes is stored in stacked, covered, plastic tubs in my storage area. Likewise, I archived all record files, post-fire by year, and stacked them in matching plastic-lidded storage containers. All tax files are stored both electronically and on paper, in two-hour-rated file cabinets. My accountant also keeps a back up copy.

Appraisals, original receipts, and photos of our more expensive household items are stored in plastic zippered envelopes in our six-hour rated safe. My home insurance agent has a copy of the disk that contains our documentation photos (described in chapter 1), and we update these annually, usually near our wedding anniversary. We also take pictures every third year, at each major holiday, to record how we move items in our home during these times. It also allows us to document what seasonal items we have. In addition, my husband keeps a back up disk of these photos off the premises, in his desk at his office.

We have our art and antiques re-appraised every five years, and we keep a photo and original appraisal of all major pieces of jewelry in our fire-rated safe. If you don't have a safe like this, keep that documentation in a safe place outside of your home. Don't make the mistake many do, and that is to tape it to the back of the artwork! Typically, you insure these items separately in a rider to your home owner's policy.

 **Key Lessons**

1. Use caution and properly ventilate computer and electronic storage devices.

2. Don't overload circuits or outlets with electronic periphery.

3. Keep appraisals current and stored in fireproof storage.

4. Store valuable books and records that are not in frequent use in plastic-lidded tubs and file holders.

Stow, Grab & Go List: Home Office or Library

_____

_____

_____

_____

_____

_____

_____

_____

_____

_____

_____

_____

_____

_____

_____

_____

_____

_____

_____

_____

_____

_____

_____

CHAPTER Eight: Bedrooms

Our safest havens. Our most private places. And perhaps the deadliest room in the house. Most deaths from fires happen when family members: a) sleep through the warning until they succumb to the smoke; or, b) smoke in bed and the mattress ignites; or, c) become trapped on upper floors with no means of safely escaping—e.g., no ladder, a window that can't be opened, or not enough protection between the fire source and them to wait for help.

💡 Bedroom Safety Tips

1. Reread the chapters that covered smoking materials (6), fire escape ladders (2), and practicing how to get out (2).

2. Consider putting smoke alarms outside each bedroom door as well as inside each bedroom. This will not only alert you to smoke in the hallway but potentially to smoke within a closed bedroom.

3. Compartmentalize your home as much as possible. Earlier we examined how different thicknesses of drywall can delay the breakthrough of a typical fire (chapter 3). Consider replacing your hollow core bedroom doors with heavier (more costly), better fire-rated, solid-core doors. When closed, the solid-core doors can add significant time for help to arrive in the event a fire traps you.

4. Sleep with those doors *closed*. By combining thicker dry wall, solid core doors, and alarms inside and outside the bedroom, you will

sleep more soundly. You're safer, and as an added bonus, less noise penetrates the space as well.

5. Finally, *never, never, never* smoke in bed. Reread this line. It's not complicated. It's not detailed. It doesn't even require a footnote. *Don't do it ever!*

🐾 Space Heaters

These appliances are most dangerous near sleeping areas and bedding. In 2005, space-heating equipment caused one-third of home heating fires in the U.S. and over 70 percent of home heating fire deaths. All types are suspect, including portable electric heaters, portable kerosene heaters, wood stoves, fireplaces with inserts, and room gas heaters.

Common causes of space heating home fires are: lack of regular cleaning, leading to creosote build-up in wood burning devices, their associated chimneys, and connectors; failure to keep space heaters an adequate distance from combustibles; basic flaws in the construction or installation of the equipment; and fueling errors involving liquid-or gas-fueled equipment.[27]

💡 Safety Tips for Space Heaters and Other Heating Apparatus [28]

1. When buying a new space heater, make sure it carries the mark of an independent testing laboratory and is legal for use in your community. (Some communities do not permit portable kerosene heaters, for example.)

2. Install your stationary (fixed) space heater according to manufacturer's instructions or applicable codes; or better yet, have it installed by a professional.

3. Plug your electric-powered space heater into an outlet with sufficient capacity and never into an extension cord.

4. Use the proper grade of the proper fuel for your liquid-fueled space heater, and never use gasoline in any heater not approved for gasoline use. Refuel only in a well-ventilated area and when the equipment is cool.

5. In your fireplace or wood stove, use only dry, seasoned wood to avoid the build-up of creosote—an oily deposit that easily catches

fire and accounts for most chimney fires and the largest share of home heating fires generally. Use only paper or kindling wood, not a flammable liquid, to start the fire. Do not use artificial logs in wood stoves.

6. Make sure your fireplace has a sturdy screen to prevent sparks from flying into the room. Allow fireplace and woodstove ashes to cool before disposing in a metal container, which is kept a safe distance from your home.

7. For coal or wood stoves or fireplaces, have a professional inspect the chimney connection and chimney, as well as other related equipment, every year, and clean this equipment as often as the inspections indicate.

8. Follow manufacturer's recommendations regarding the operation of space heaters, and turn off space heaters whenever the room they are in is unoccupied. You should turn portable space heaters off when you go to bed because you can easily knock them over in the dark; but make sure your primary heating equipment for the bedroom is sufficient to avoid risks to residents from severe cold.

9. Vent fuel-burning equipment to the outside, keep the venting clear and unobstructed, and properly seal the exit point around the vent, making sure deadly carbon monoxide does not build up in the home.

10. Refill portable kerosene heaters in a well-ventilated area, away from flames and other heat sources, and only when the device has cooled completely. Use only the type of kerosene specified by the manufacturer. Be sure to check to see if your community allows such heaters.

11. Adequately ventilate any gas-fueled heating device. Unventilated gas space heaters in bedrooms or bathrooms must be small and wall mounted. Never use liquefied petroleum (LP) gas heaters with self contained fuel supplies inside the home.

💡 Protecting the Bedroom's Contents

A good rule of thumb: if you're not wearing it, using it, or looking for it, pick *it* up and put *it* away. Clutter, dust, and accumulations of paper all pose a high fire risk when near any electrical or heat source—like lamps, extension cords, radiators, room space heaters, fireplaces, or candles.

Store your off-season clothing, neatly folded, into plastic, lidded, storage tubs. Now, if you do have a fire, the water and smoke won't penetrate, and you'll only be replacing half of your wardrobe. I recommend shoebox size, locking-lid, plastic containers in which to store your shoes for smoke and water protection. They make your shoes last longer, stay cleaner, and the containers stack great. Plus, you can see through the container to identify the pair of shoes you need.

I have another story for you. My old colonial home had only one small closet in each bedroom, so, when my daughter married and moved out, I converted one of the two attic bedrooms into a giant walk-in closet. Through a series of hooks, racks, suspended poles, and shelves, I fashioned a closet that housed nearly every article of clothing that I possessed. Tucked into the center, I placed a floor standing jewelry box. It held my few valuable pieces of jewelry and loads of costume jewelry.

During the fire, flames rapidly penetrated the soffits along the roofline, spread throughout the roof structure, and travelled down the walls surrounding the central chimney and the house's core, causing the roof to be fully lost in a matter of hours. As the fire spread, and water fell on the exposed third floor, these racks of heavy, soggy clothing fell to the floor. I later learned that this crazy closet served as a protective layer to both my jewelry box and its contents. I would later learn that this closet full of wet clothing also protected a small section of the master bedroom below.

When we were safely able to return to the house, mid-day on Saturday, you can imagine my delight in finding my most valuable pieces of jewelry—very dirty, but—in one piece, under this pile of destroyed clothing. The costume jewelry had changed its composition beyond salvage, but any genuine silver or gold items cleaned up with elbow grease and soap. My husband and daughter teamed up and spent several hours at her kitchen sink on this task. Both found great satisfaction in restoring something from the remains.

Miracles Everywhere

It's hard to imagine on one side of this devastation (just below the "closet" room) sat three pieces of treasured heirlooms—a hand carved teak foot locker over one hundred fifty years old that had made the voyage from Canton, China, when my mother-in-law's father emigrated at the turn of the century; and a one hundred year old loveseat and rocker, given to me by my mother, a gift from her grandmother upon her passing, when I was eighteen years old. The picture below shows you the devastation of the room these three items were in.

Yet to my surprise, the fire restoration company (Action Fire Restoration, Chicopee, MA), salvaged and restored these three pieces of sooty and scarred furniture. It took them nearly six months, but they were able to sand down the wood elements, refinish the wood, and re-upholster the fabric areas of these items. It took nearly three months of work to simply get the smoke out of the wood.

Similarly, I had about ten pieces of art created in oils, by family members, which were not in the fire's path, but heavily blackened by soot and water. The restoration company shook their heads, so I called the owner of a small picture framing business that I had driven past a hundred times. The owner agreed to come by and take the pieces. He asked me if they had value beyond sentimental, and I said no. He said, "Let me see what I can do. Come by in a few weeks and if I'm successful, just buy your new frames from me."

Thanks to Jeff of Jeff's Picture Framing in Springfield, MA, I have those original oils cleaned, sealed and framed, and hanging throughout my new home. And, as you can guess, Jeff received all of my framing business from that point forward.

As a closing thought, you can't practice escaping from the bedroom often enough. Be sure your family has practiced at least two ways of getting out, and be sure each bedroom has its own means of calling for help, whether it's a ten dollar extension phone or a cell phone for each individual family member. Be sure that anyone can, and knows how to, get help in an emergency.

 **Key Lessons**

1. Don't smoke in bed, ever.

2. Compartmentalize bedrooms with closed, solid core doors, and install smoke detectors both inside and outside the rooms.

3. Use space heaters with great caution.

4. Store clothing, shoes, and personal belongings that are not in season, safely out of harm's way by placing them in lidded, rubber, or plastic storage tubs.

Stow, Grab & Go List: Bedrooms

_____

_____

_____

_____

_____

_____

_____

_____

_____

_____

_____

_____

_____

_____

_____

_____

_____

_____

_____

_____

_____

_____

_____

_____

_____

• •

CHAPTER NINE: LAUNDRY, ATTICS, CELLARS

Not very glamorous, and by measure, not as dangerous as one might imagine, these rooms do however pose some hazards, and in the event of a fire, can actually be a source of fuel.

 **Laundry**

Some of us have dedicated laundry rooms in different areas of our homes. One of my homes had one located off my kitchen, next to my back entrance and garage access. I've had homes with the laundry room between the kitchen and dining room, or on the second floor between bedrooms and bathrooms. Yet another had it housed in my open cellar, along one wall. Regardless of its location, the hazards remain: water from the washer and its hoses, and fire in the dryer from the lint that can accumulate. Most manufacturers recommend that you replace the connector water hoses to your washing machine every five years. Turn the water off to these hoses when departing your home, whether on vacation or just for a long weekend. This takes the pressure off the fastener and greatly reduces the risk of the hose rupturing and flooding your space.

Between 1999 and 2002, there was an average of 13,300 clothes dryer fires annually in U.S. homes.[29] Wherever yours is, consider these safety measures: [30]

1. Do not operate the dryer without a lint filter. Clean lint filters before or after each use and remove accumulated lint from around the drum. Dryer lint is highly combustible and causes your dryer to lose efficiency. A good friend of mine, who was a volunteer fire fighter, related tale after tale of flaming dryers whose owners had never emptied the lint baskets.

2. Make sure you plug the dryer into an outlet suitable for its electrical needs, as overloaded electrical outlets can result in blown fuses or tripped circuit breakers.

3. Don't store combustibles—like clean or dirty clothes, rags, cleaning supplies—on top of or near your dryer.

4. Turn the dryer off when leaving the house.

5. Have your dryer and washer serviced and repaired by a licensed professional.

6. Have gas powered dryers inspected by a professional regularly to ensure the gas line and connection are intact.

7. There are no dryer gremlins. If you've lost a sock, it's probably under, behind, or between your washer, dryer, and a wall. Move your appliances out at least quarterly to find these items that could catch fire.

8. Locate a smoke alarm outside the laundry room. (*Funny story...I have a whole house alarm system, including glass break alarms; and we have one of these just outside the laundry room. Without fail, I will set the alarm for the night and then go in to finish the laundry, forgetting the alarm is on. I'll open the dryer, fold the last load, and shut the dryer door, only to activate the glass break alarm! Ugh!*)

Cellars and Attics

We use these areas as our storage facilities, workrooms, catchall, and sometimes living spaces. If you use these spaces as bedrooms, reread that chapter (8). If your attic is a bedroom, be sure you have ladders to extend from a window that is large enough from which to escape in the event of an emergency evacuation. If your bedroom is in the cellar, make sure you have a window or door to the outside that you, guests, or family members can adequately use as an escape.

If you use these areas primarily for storage, be sure you reread the sections on safe storage of flammables (chapter 9), and consider placing items you store in lidded, plastic, or rubber tubs. Some of us use these areas as work rooms and often use power equipment and tools in these rooms. Here are some important safety tips.

Cellars, Power Equipment, and Tools [31]

- Always unplug power tools when they are not in use.
- Keep work areas free from dust, wood shavings, and other hazardous materials.
- Keep fire and heat sources away from craft areas, wood working spaces, or other flammable work spaces.
- Be sure to use cooler, safer, fluorescent bulbs in your moveable light sources.
- Keep items stored in air tight containers including paints, brushes, solvents, rags, and other items that might easily feed a fire.
- Store cleaning products, paints, solvents, and other liquids in appropriate cabinets away from children and heat sources. Always read and follow manufacturer's warnings on labels as they relate to the safe storage of these items.
- Keep items away from furnaces, air conditioners, water heaters, and in-home fuel storage tanks, pumps, or filters.
- If you have exposed walls or ceilings where electrical, phone, or cable wires are evident and connections are visible, be sure to keep these areas free of dust and combustibles, and out of the reach of children.
- Inspect both attic and cellar for evidence of rodents and pests. Raccoons in rural areas are particularly invasive in attics and can gnaw through electrical wires—a frequent cause of attic fires in these locations. We suspect that in our case, a field mouse or chipmunk may have been the cause of an arc in that knob and tube wiring in the ceiling of our exterior porch—we'll never know for sure.

 **Key Lessons**

1. Check the hoses on your washing machine and replace them every five years.

2. Clean the dryer filter after every load.

3. Clean the vent to the outside at least twice a year to remove built up dust.

4. Tend to all indoor work and storage spaces and never store flammables near your major home appliances.

5. If a family member occupies an attic or cellar bedroom, practice escaping the same to assure adequate window access.

Stow, Grab & Go List: Laundry, Attic and Cellar

CHAPTER TEN: GARAGE AND OUTDOOR SPACES

Attached and detached garages require the same consideration. Both can be a source of fire, and fire from either can spread to your home. A fire can start in a garage from a couple of sources. Power tools, portable heating sources, flammable liquids, damaging rodents, an idling automobile, and careless use and disposal of smoking materials can all lead to a fire in or around your garage.

To better protect your home and yourself, follow these steps[32]:

1. Never leave your automobile, tractors, or other motorized engines running, or idling, in a closed garage. Not only can carbon monoxide quickly accumulate and cause major health concerns, but these gas fired engines also throw off extreme levels of heat which can quickly cause a fire.

2. Enclose your attached garage walls with a double layer of five-eighths-inch drywall to further separate your home from a fire that may start within this space. (This includes ceilings! Our last two homes have had the master bedroom right over the garage.)

3. Don't stack or store combustibles in or near your garage. Stack firewood away from all buildings and dwellings. Similarly, recycle newspapers, cardboard, and other combustibles in fire safe containers away from your home and garage.

4. Keep that outdoor grill outdoors and away from any structure, roofline overhangs, or awnings. Don't grill in a closed garage or within the

three walls of an open garage unless you have at least another eight-foot clearance from the fire source to the nearest overhead structure (including the overhead door!).

5. Never store a hot grill next to the structure. Allow enough time for the grill to cool completely before emptying coals, or moving it into a shelter or adjacent to a structure. Dispose of those embers and coals only after they have cooled completely and only in appropriate containers. Do not place these coals in the trash or other combustible containers.

6. Treat outdoor fireplaces and fire pits as you would indoor fireplaces. Only burn wood appropriate to the size and shape of the container. Never ignite a fire using gasoline, kerosene, or other flammable liquids. Always check wind velocity and direction before lighting these fires, making sure that conditions will not cause hot embers to reach your home, garage, or nearby structure. Keep a water source or extinguisher nearby in case these conditions change suddenly.

 **Propane Safety**[33]

Note: Propane is the most common form of Liquefied Petroleum (LP) gas. Butane is another LP gas.

- Handle any propane-powered equipment cautiously and always follow the manufacturer's instructions. Cylinder tanks for equipment such as stoves and ovens must be located outside of the home.

- Never store or use propane gas cylinders larger than one pound inside the home.

- Never operate a propane-powered gas grill inside the home.

- Have propane gas equipment inspected periodically by a professional for possible leaks or malfunctioning parts.

- Carefully follow the manufacturer's instructions when lighting a pilot.

- If you smell a strong odor of gas, leave the area immediately and call your fire department from outside the home.

💡 Key Lessons

1. Never store combustibles in your garage or home.

2. Use caution with outdoor grills, their hot coals, and their proximity to your home or garage.

3. Treat outdoor fireplaces and fire pits as you would an indoor fireplace.

Stow, Grab & Go List: Garage

_____

_____

_____

_____

_____

_____

_____

_____

_____

_____

_____

_____

_____

_____

_____

_____

_____

_____

_____

_____

_____

_____

_____

_____

_____

_____

CHAPTER ELEVEN: How Can *YOU* Help?

Someone you know or care about has just had a major fire or loss, and you want to help. Our friends and family felt so helpless in those early days. I couldn't tell them what I needed; no one could.

 Well, *now* I can make a few suggestions.

1. Reach out. Hug them. Tell them how terrible this is; but reinforce how happy you are that they are unhurt and alive. It's not trite. It's wonderful to look into the eyes of your family and friends and see and *feel* the sincerity in those words.

2. Fast action is required if you are to save photos. Take these items and clean, dry, and sort them. We didn't have a space to lay all these out, and hours mattered. We were able to restore all but the photos on the walls by having friends who acted quickly.

3. Find out what was lost. In our case it was easy: everything, nearly. My friends knew I had a passion for cooking, so every time we gathered, they brought me a cookbook to replace the ones I lost. One friend even had a girls' night martini party and instead of bringing the hostess a gift, each friend brought me their favorite cookbook. Finally, anyone who had ever gotten a recipe from me in the past recopied it and sent it back to me. There are no words to describe how all this made me feel except my favorite: *overwhelmed.*

4. Another friend went out and put together a home clean-up kit with cleaning rags, towels, pails, mops, brooms, sponges, detergents, and more. While we couldn't really use these in the devastated house, we needed all of this as we moved into our rental place. When you have to shop to replace everything, it was nice not to have to go buy cleaning supplies.

5. Another group of friends got together and bought us a bedside CD player/alarm clock with a generous gift card for music. The attached greeting card read something to the effect "we want to bring the music back to your days and nights" and it allowed us to begin replacing our music collection.

6. One acquaintance from work, Terry G., had her daughter drive her to the nearest dress store where she proceeded to buy two outfits of clothes for me. It seems she had admired my clothing from afar at work for years, and she just wanted to be sure that I had a start on replacing my wardrobe; a kindness I'll never forget. Another longtime friend, our realtor in fact, brought me a beautiful sweater. She said "I love this sweater so much that I bought two! I want you to have this one."

7. Under my son's instigation, our family began pooling their collective family photos and videos, recreating some of those moments we had lost. It was nice when that box arrived with these hand selected memories of me, my children, my wedding, their wedding, my parents, my cousins, my brother, and their families, my husband and his family. Even my golfing buddies began copying our team photos from over the years to replace these. *Overwhelmed.*

8. We had two dogs at the time of the fire, and had installed in our New England home a special motorized, electronic dog door, just like the one we had installed previously in our home in Arizona. The dogs wore a magnet on their collar and walked up to the door. We switched the door on, and when the dogs stood in front of the door, it raised, the dogs entered or exited, and then the door closed. The one in our kitchen, after the fire, seemed unharmed except for the smoke stains on the plexi-glass door. We took it out of the wall in its entirety prior to the house's demolition, had it boxed for shipping and wrote a letter to the manufacturer describing what had happened. We asked the manufacturer to check the mechanisms and replace the plexi-glass, call us with the amount this would cost so we could give them a credit card to cover the repairs and return shipping expense.

We then shipped it off to Solo Pet Doors. Two weeks later, a brand new pet door arrived with this note:

> Mr. Quinn,
>
>> I am so sorry for your loss. Rather than risk using a possibly damaged door, please accept this new replacement as my gift to you. I am happy that you, your family, and your beloved dogs survived this tragedy.

Once again—overwhelmed.

9. Want to help strangers? Consider volunteering or making a cash contribution to your local chapter of the American Red Cross. This great organization relies upon your time and donations to help others in times of disaster; from those that affect just one family, to those touching entire neighborhoods, communities, or regions.

No matter what you do, the kindness, compassion, and love will always show through. This is true in any tragedy, and when you feel overwhelmed with the magnitude of the loss, it's balancing when the loving-kindness of family, friends, and strangers overwhelms you.

Interesting Encounters While Replacing Our Wardrobes

Shortly after the fire, we needed to get back to our jobs. We had been away for our wedding and honeymoon for almost four weeks, and had only returned to our jobs for five days when the fire occurred. After the fire, we spent the first full week putting together an inventory of our losses, trying to assess and record the damage (fully, sun up to sun down, each day) as we raced against time and the decay that occurs after the fire—when water and the elements take over. We were approaching the weekend and still only had the jeans and t-shirts we purchased to do this messy work. We had to hit the stores and use that advance insurance check.

We had mixed experiences. That Saturday, my husband and I went into the local Chico's store (where I had shopped periodically). We told the manager what had occurred and she immediately wheeled out an empty rack, put one of everything in my size on it grouped into "outfits", set up a changing room and said "try what you like, and if you are too tired, take it home and try it. Keep the hangers, keep what you want. Bring in the tags and we'll settle the bill then." Her kindness and thoughtfulness overwhelmed me. You can imagine that I have become a customer of that store (and Chico's as well) for life!

My husband, however, had a different experience. Some background. Prior to the wedding, we had frequented this prominent local men's store to purchase gifts and to make winter wardrobe additions to my husband's armada since he had just moved to New England from Arizona. In fact, in the months before our wedding, he ordered a custom shirt and very expensive Italian tuxedo from this store for his wedding suit. Each time, we worked with the same salesman, who recognized us now by site.

On the Sunday immediately after our fire, my husband drove to the store, alone, and waited in the lot for this store to open. He remembered a green summer weight suit they had, by a designer whose sizes always fit him, and the last time he had been in, it had been on sale. He said to me as he left, "I don't really feel like shopping, so I'll grab it if it's still there, get it hemmed, and at least have one suit for work when I go back. Then, I can go in after work one night and pick out the rest of my wardrobe."

When the store opened, he went right to the rack and there was the suit. No longer on sale, (hard to understand as it was the last one of its kind) but there. Now, remember he needed everything: belts, shoes, socks, underwear, shirts, slacks, suits, ties. He found his salesman, shared the story of the past twenty-four hours and the salesman just looked at him. My husband said, "So let's start with this suit. It's a particular label, I know it will fit and only requires hemming; and, before I left for our wedding trip, it was on sale!" The salesman said (I kid you not), "Well (chuckling) it's not now!" He didn't offer to help him in any way. He didn't say "Mr. Quinn, sit over here. Let me get you a coffee and let me see what we have in your size and to your liking. Then, I'll call the owner and see what we can do." Needless to say, my husband stormed out in his t-shirt, jeans, and borrowed shoes, never to return again. I can assure you, he shared the story of this cavalier, greedy salesman with everyone he encountered. They lost more than one customer that day.

Thanks to our friends, Laura and Joanne, who heard him tell this story, a few days later, he met—not one but two—store owners of area men's stores who treated him as Chico's treated me; and, they became regular haunts for him for many seasons to come.

 **Key Lessons**

1. Reach out—you can help.

2. No act of kindness is too small.

3. Get personal—if this is your friend or family member, do something personal. If they are strangers, go to an agency, like the local chapter of the American Red Cross, and make a donation designated to help that family. They'll see to it the family gets it, and puts it to good use.

EPILOGUE

Time has passed—six years actually. We've moved away from New England and now reside in a mid-Atlantic state. I had the chance this past summer to drive past the old spot. It no longer resembles the disaster I remember.

On 9/11/2002, while the church bells tolled on the first anniversary of one of the most terrifying days in our country's history, bulldozers leveled what remained of the fire-damaged structure. The family who purchased the vacant lot from us has now completed construction of their dream home. Some neighbors have passed away, a few have moved, and many remain. A few recall as I do the details of that fire, and the days and weeks that followed.

In our home, we will speak of it when we go to look for something and then try to recall, "Was that a pre- or post-fire possession?" We sometimes talk about it when the extended family gathers and my nephews ask me to recall the details once again, so they can see it all in their minds' eyes. (Those firefighters...)

And as I put the finishing touches to what I hope will be a helpful reference tool for you, I find that this writing exercise has been cathartic. I am closing this chapter of my life—the one with disaster but no tragedy—to pursue life's next challenge.

I wish you each well and the safe, peaceful enjoyment of your home, your sanctuary. Be sure to thank the realtor, insurance agent, banker, friend, or family member who gave this guide to you. Who knows, it may just save your stuff or maybe, your life!

I am donating a portion of the proceeds from the sale of this guide in the name of all firefighters to the National Fire Prevention Association, whose research was a great resource and invaluable reference to my work. Another portion will go to the Pioneer Valley Chapter of the American Red Cross to help others overcome disaster.

ACKNOWLEDGEMENTS

Putting a book together like this one requires the help and contributions of many. So does surviving a fire like ours. I'd like to officially say thank you to those who helped us.

First, to my brother, Christopher, who is always at the other end of that phone when we need him. He not only suggested resources, provided technical assistance, and emotional support, but he actually gave up a day of site seeing in Italy to do the first read of this book, and his expertise guided much of the prevention and fire safety you see here. He is and will always be my personal hero.

Next, I want to recognize Eric H. Madison, Fire Chief, Longmeadow Fire Department, Longmeadow, MA, who spent several hours meeting with me as I began the research for this book. And, of course, on that fateful morning, for all his comforting words and encouraging support of us. He leads a great team of firefighters in that quiet western Massachusetts community.

Dennis Berry, Secretary of the Corporation and Licensing for the National Fire Protection Association, for his help and the help of his research team in their review of this work and their permission to use their statistics and tips throughout this book. Their researchers and authors spent countless hours organizing and covering these facts and statistics, and as a practice, create very helpful safety tips for consumers. You can find more of their work on their website, http://www.nfpa.org.

Special thanks to Reverend Larry Provenzano, LFD Chaplain and pastor of Saint Andrews Episcopal Church, Longmeadow, MA, and Rick Lee, Executive Director, and his team at the Pioneer Valley Chapter of the American Red Cross who comforted us and stayed with us during the fire and for many hours after.

We could never have finished our inventory or kept our sanity during that first week without the loving help and guidance of Scott Patton, friend and member of the Action Fire Restoration team, Chicopee, MA. And, a huge thanks to the skilled team at Action Fire Restoration who salvaged three precious heirlooms that we can now leave to my granddaughters.

Heartfelt thanks to our daughter, Cory, and her husband, Aaron, who gave us a bed, meals, and constant love and support throughout the days, weeks, and months following the fire, even if our first week of sleeping in their house included my tall husband, myself, our two Schnauzers and their St. Bernard all sharing one full sized bed!

Thanks to our son, Brant, who was a thousand miles away, feeling pretty helpless. With his technical savvy, he coordinated the compilation of family photos, videos, and assorted memory gathering (like senior portraits, key family photos from weddings, etc.), leading the charge to replace what had been lost.

Jane Palmer, realtor extraordinaire and friend, who found us refuge and so much more. We were in a lovely rental home within a week or so, and actively looking for our next permanent home within the month. She became our neighbor, and will always be our friend.

Our adjuster from Hanover Insurance Company, Rick (I'll protect his identity), Worcester, MA, who at every turn really was there for us. He made sure we had what we needed at all times.

Jeff Cohen of Jeff's Picture Framing, Springfield, MA, who so kindly took those wet, smelly, dirty oil paintings and found a way to give us back precious paintings from my mom and son.

Thanks to our close friends, Tony, Joan, Loring, Nancy, Tom, Fran, Mike, and Judy who took those nasty, wet, sooty photos home and returned to us dry, clean, and saved memories

Our employers, who were also friends, who gave us the time we needed to sort it all out, and the friendship we needed both on the day of the fire, and for the long weeks that followed. They brought clothing, gifts, and acts of kindness that will always be treasured.

And lastly, our dear neighbors who contributed jackets, shoes, (bathrooms while we worked to make sense out of the mess remaining) and more emotional support than I can put into words along the way; especially Joanne, Michael, Bonnie, Alan, Ron, Ginny, Tim, Trish, Ron, Jeff, Carl, Joe, Judy, George, Ann, all of their families, and so many others.

APPENDIX A—PROTECTION ITEMS
SHOPPING LIST

Visit www.isurvivedahousefire.com *for virtual shopping links and examples of items listed here.*

• Rubber or plastic tubs (various sizes) with locking lids (preferably water tight). *Wal-Mart®, K-Mart®, Target®, The Container Store®, Home Depot®, Lowe's®, etc.* *

• Rubber or plastic file size storage containers for those old and current records. *Staples®, Office Max®, other office supply, and general merchandise stores cited above.* *

• Plastic storage bags with water/air tight zippered closures (multiple sizes, including very large bags). *Grocery centers and general merchandise stores.* *

• Two-hour fire rated file cabinet and if you can afford it, a six-hour fire rated safe. *Office supply stores listed above, home improvement stores, hardware stores, locksmith's and safe distributors.* *

• Shoebox size lidded plastic storage containers. *See plastic tub sources.*

• CD plastic storage containers. *Music stores, general merchandise stores.* *

• Fire escape ladders for all second and third story bedrooms (or attic space if using it for anything other than storage). *Home improvement centers, and see online links.* *

• Plastic outlet covers and plug protectors if you have small children in the house. *Home improvement centers, Babies-R-Us®, Toys-R-Us®, electrical supply stores, hardware stores.* *

• Off the floor storage shelves designed to hold the shape and size tubs you've purchased. I recommend steel or plastic. *Home improvement centers, general merchandise stores.* *

*not intended to be an all inclusive list of potential retail locations; these are just handy references

Appendix B—Creating Your Post Loss Inventory to File a Claim

The following pages are simple Excel spreadsheets that I created to document our loss. If you use the two pages as a workbook, adding additional pages like page two, you will have a single interactive file with these very handy references. Since our fire, I have received several calls for copies of it. Here are the pages as I set them up. I hope you *never* need it.

If you would like the actual Excel spread sheet file version with calculators, visit my website at www.isurvivedahousefire.com. You can download it there.

Summary Sheet

Room	Quantity (Item Count)	Replacement Cost	Adjustment Amount	Discounted Pay Out Amount	Cost to Repair
1st Floor Bath					$0.00
Cellar Bath					$0.00
Master Bath - 2nd Floor					$0.00
Attic - Room One					$0.00
Attic - Linen & Hallway Closet					$0.00
Attic - Bedroom #2					$0.00
Cellar					$0.00
Master Bedroom					$0.00
Guest Bedroom -2nd Floor					$0 00
Home Office 2nd Floor					$0.00
Study					$0.00
Dining Room					$0.00
Living Room					$0.00
Kitchen					$0.00
Front Hall - Entry					$0.00
Family Room - Cellar					$0.00
Side Porch - Yard					$0.00
Totals	0	$0.00	-$	$0.00	$0.00

Repeat this page for every room in the dwelling.

Item Description/Name	Quantity	Approximate Date of Purchase	Replacement Cost or Purchase Price	Adjustment Amount* to be completed by Insurance Company	Discounted Pay Out Amount	Cost to Repair
					$0.00	
					$0.00	
					$0.00	
					$0.00	
					$0.00	
					$0.00	
					$0.00	
					$0.00	
					$0.00	
					$0.00	
					$0.00	
			$0.00		$0.00	$0.00

Appendix C: Top Ten Things I Want To Get Out First

1. Myself, Family and Pets

2.

3.

4.

5.

6.

7.

8.

9.

10. A change of clothing that fits me (complete with shoes, jacket, and undergarments!)

REFERENCES

see also www.isurvivedahousefire.com for these links and more

1 Karter, Michael J., Jr., Fire Loss in the United States During 2006, September, 2007

2 Ahrens, Marty, Home Structure Fires, September, 2007

3 ibid

4 ibid

5 www.nfpa.org/smokealarms

6 ibid

7 ibid

8 Hall, John R., Jr. US Experience with sprinklers and other automatic fire extinguishing equipment, June, 2007

9 ibid

10 http://en.wikipedia.org/wiki/Framing_%28construction%29

11 Ahrens, Marty, Home Structure Fires, September, 2007

12 http://www.nfpa.org/itemDetsail.asp?categoryID=285&itemID=19048&URL=Research%20&%20Reports/Fact%20sheets/Electrical%20safety/Elictrical%20circuit-interrupters

13 Ahrens, Marty, Home Structure Fires, September, 2007

14 ibid

15 http://www.nfpa.org

16 ibid

17 http://ga.water.usgs.gov/edu/sc4.html

18 http://www.nfpa.org/Candles

19 ibid

20 ibid

21 Ahrens, Marty, Home Structure Fires, September, 2007

22 Hall, John R., Home Structure Fires involving electrical distribution or lighting equipment, March 2008

23 http://www.nfpa.org/research/nfpafactsheets/electrical/

24 http://www.nfpa.org/research/NFPAFactSheets/holiday

25 www.barnhardt.net & www.ncfi.com ; DuPont Corporation web PowerPoint for Kevlar.

26 DuPont Corporation web PowerPoint for Kevlar.

27 Hall, John R., Home Structure Fires involving heating equipment, November, 2007

28 http://www.nfpa.org/research/factsheets/heatingequipment

29 Hall, John R., U.S. Home Product Report, Appliances & Equipment, November, 2005

30 http://www.nfpa.org/research/factsheets/appliances/dryer

31 http://www.nfpa.org/research/factsheets

32 ibid

33 http://www.nfpa.org/research/nfpafactsheets/propanesafety

About the Author

Candace Quinn earned a Master's degree from Northwestern University and a Bachelor's degree from Rockford College. She is a consultant, author, and speaker within the healthcare industry. She resides in Northern Virginia with her husband, Michael, and is a mother of two and grandmother of five.

Printed in the United States
220200BV00001B/9/P